A writer, educator, artist, and musician, Kay Harkins lives in San Diego, California. Retired from a career teaching writing and literature, she continues to collaborate with other writers, artists, and musicians and tends to her rose garden, her rescued greyhound Lazarus, and the home she shares with her husband, to whom she has been married for over fifty years. She holds an MFA from Bennington College in Bennington, Vermont.

For Alice DeBerry Kane, Bennington's best gift.

Kay Harkins

QUEEN OF THE LEAVES

A MEMOIR OF LOST AND FOUND

AUSTIN MACAULEY PUBLISHERS™

LONDON • CAMBRIDGE • NEW YORK • SHARJAH

Ordering Information:
Quantity sales: special discounts are available on quantity purchases by corporations, associations, and others. For details, contact the publisher at the address below.

Publisher's Cataloging-in-Publication data
Harkins, Kay
Queen of the Leaves

ISBN 9781645369325 (Paperback)
ISBN 9781645369318 (Hardback)
ISBN 9781645369349 (ePub e-book)

Library of Congress Control Number: 2020905175

www.austinmacauley.com/us

First Published (2020)
Austin Macauley Publishers LLC
40 Wall Street, 28th Floor
New York, NY 10005
USA

mail-usa@austinmacauley.com
+1 (646) 5125767

I wish to acknowledge the writers who educated, challenged, and supported me in the writing of this book, beginning with Dr. Arthur Seamans, who first believed in me as a writer and who has never flagged in his encouragement. I owe tremendous gratitude to writers Richard Bausch, Sven Birkerts, Susan Cheever, Lucy Grealy (of blessed memory), George Packer, and Scott Cairns, whose teaching and philosophies of writing offered me invaluable tools in my life in the arts.

Without my writing companions, some of whom were my students, I could not have seen this project to completion. With both tough love and compassion, they never let me give up. My profound thanks to Alice DeBerry Kane, Mame Willey (of blessed memory), Danielle Cervantes Stephens, Brandyn Jennings, Katie Manning, Gaelan and Megan Gilbert, Aly Lewis, Jennifer Hartenburg, Michele Marr, George Tsoris, and John Bonadeo.

To my fellow survivors, my sisters, Janis and Susan, my grandparents, my husband's family, and my children, Cadence and Bryan, go endless thanks for their inspiration, patience, and the blessing of their love. To my beloved husband, Jack, I owe my life itself.

Chapter One
Father Lost

Somewhere between the incantations of Latin, Sister Miriam's story time, and the black and white Life of Christ films at St. Theresa's School, I began to expect an immediate return of Jesus Christ.

During the months before Easter, the year I turned six, I would roll all the way over against the wall at night before I went to sleep, in case He came in the middle of the night, and finding Himself tired, would have a welcome place to sleep. I fluffed up the pillow and put my head on just one half of it. Lying there next to the cool wall, I flipped the sheet up into the air and let it float down to create a barely perceptible breeze. That must be *the way it is in heaven,* I thought, *everything cozy and soft and just a whisper of sweet wind keeping everything fresh.*

Sometimes I'd plan what we'd do when I found Him there in the morning, usually deciding to let Him sleep in a little, then waking Him up in time for breakfast. I imagined taking His hand and leading Him out into our living room, how surprised my mother and father would be. His robes would be white and worn out from a thousand washings, like my sheets, and would smell like incense on Easter morning.

I perplexed my mother, those few months or so, saving a portion of everything on my plate, just in case Jesus came during a meal. It did not occur to me that if Jesus Christ arrived at 6000 College Street, Des Moines, Iowa, in the Year of Our Lord, 1952, my mother would have set a place for Him, so private was my fantasy. I put off eating what I saved for him on my plate as long as I could.

"You will sit there till you eat it," she or my father would say, as I sat swinging my legs under the chair, waiting it out for as long as I could.

Sometimes, a hand would be put to my forehead or questions about tummy-troubles would arise, but my good cheer and enthusiasm-for-play did not diminish, so they assumed willful fickleness of appetite. After a while, I decided that Jesus would not want to eat the cold food, so I had to gag it down.

Although the Lord's return had probably broken into my imagination from some Lenten discipline at St. Theresa's, my mother didn't link my behavior at the table to theology. Not understanding the Second Coming enough myself to explain it to my mother, I was afraid she might laugh at me.

She had converted to Catholicism in order to marry my father, but she took little delight in the rituals of Catholicism, having come from a family of non-practicing Episcopalians. I do not ever recall seeing her pray the rosary, and neither she nor my father seemed to have much interest in going to church, saying prayers or helping me study my catechism.

My father's mother, Helen, ensured my weekly attendance at church, and who had observed my fascination with icons and statuary, had been the one to nurture my affinity for religious life.

"Paul, come in here," I overheard my mother call to my father one Saturday morning. In my room, she'd discovered my toy box covered with a sheet and set with a prayer book, my blue child's rosary, and a plastic 'glow in the dark' cross that I'd won as some prize at school. I started to step from behind the bathroom door when she winked at him and smiled, wiggling a crooked finger, but something stopped me.

"She's got her own altar in here."

My father shook his head and smiled, "She's her grandma's little girl."

"Don't you think this is a little too much?"

"Oh, she's a kid. She'll grow out of it. Don't forget that she wants to be a Broadway dancer."

"Yes, but she thinks she wants to be a nun too!"

"A singing, dancing nun!" I said, stepping out from the bathroom behind them. Long before the days of The Flying Nun or the Singing Nun, I believed all things were possible. I wanted to defend my shrine, but found no words.

"You have a good imagination, honey," my father said. "Let her play, Ruth. It's not hurting anything."

My good imagination felt quite valuable to me at that moment.

It was during those weeks of religious fervor that my mother was expecting her third baby, and my two-year-old sister, Janis, and I would take turns in spending weekends with our grandparents; staying first one week with our mother's parents, and the next with our father's.

Our mother needed her rest, and we welcomed the spoiling always waiting for us at our grandparents' homes.

The richest weekends came when just one of us went to each place and I would find myself riding the bus with Grandma Helen on a Sunday morning, to her large downtown church with its consequential, stained glass windows, every interior crevice imbued with incense.

My grandmother let me use her missal and prayer book with its thin, crispy pages printed in red and black, most of the gold worn off their edges. The priest always sang or spoke in Latin, but she told me her book had the words he was singing or saying in English. I could barely read at all, but that made no difference. I held the missal and pretended I was reading the things I learned at school, about the Ten Commandments, and Moses and Mary. I especially liked the part about how God never stopped loving anybody, no matter how bad they were.

In those same months of obsession, I devised my own system of penance. When I felt really bad about something I had done, I went outside and pulled my fingernails over an aluminum trash can lid. I hated the way the little prickly sounds bumped under my nails and went right up my arm into my ear. I came up with that penance one afternoon, after my mother had put me in the hall closet for doing something bad. I cannot quite remember the infraction because what I did in the closet seemed much worse to me.

My mother would always send me to the coat closet until the 'bad little Mary Kay was sorry and the good little Mary Kay would come out.' I was so indignant at being in the closet that particular occasion that I stood in there for a long time. I could not make myself feel sorry for what I'd done. The closet door was never locked, and I never felt frightened to be in there.

Often, it served as a good place to think things over and ponder the mystery of slowly being able to see things in the dark. Once my eyes had become adjusted to the darkness, I noticed a pair of Mother's shoes on the closet floor. Unable to make myself be sorry for anything, I spat into her shoes. Then, there was something to be sorry for.

"The bad little Mary Kay is sorry and the good little Mary Kay is ready to come out!" came my call.

Soon, my mother opened the door. She had a peanut butter and jelly sandwich and a smile ready for me. I gave her a big hug and took my sandwich to the back steps to eat in the sunshine after my minutes in the dark.

Getting down to the last two bites, I thought about Jesus coming back, but a glance into the sky, clear and blue, offered no sign of Him. I waited a few minutes, studying the strata of the sandwich, thinking about getting to go to confession before my first holy communion, about sitting in that big, dark booth, and telling the priest about spitting into my mother's shoes. *What would he tell me to do? Five 'Hail Mary's,' ten times through the rosary? No, I wouldn't mind that; it should be something most unpleasant, something to think twice about having to do again.*

Just then, the kid from down the street came careening by on his tricycle and knocked over the trashcan. The lid rolled around and settled down like a nickel that had been flicked across a table. I looked into the sky once more and stuffed the rest of the sandwich into my mouth.

"Watch what you're doing, ninny!" I called with my mouth full, as he sped through the alley. *Thank goodness the can was empty.*

The lid slid out of my hand as I picked it up, my nails scraping along its surface. That bad, shivery chill went up into my ear. Putting the lid back on, I tried a few scrapes just to see how much I could take.

Now, if somebody wanted to punish me, I thought, *this would mean something.* Trying ten times, then five times more, confirmed fifteen scrapes as a good basic penance, which might be worth asking about at our next catechism class.

Punishment, at least the kind I'd experienced in my six-year-old world, made perfect sense to me. My father thought I was a smart girl; he praised my singing and dancing, my drawings, laughed at my silly jokes, but my mother was best impressed with good behavior. It seemed only reasonable that corrections, in their proper measure, could be effective in achieving goodness and smartness, and were good preparation for that perfect place heaven might be.

Before I could explore any more of my punishment theories, however, Palm Sunday arrived. On that afternoon, the parish priest came around in his black car to all the homes in the parish and blessed them, sprinkling the living room with holy water from large palm fronds, which he left in the home.

The last year, we had put them up over the mirror behind the davenport. Waiting, kneeling in the rocking chair in front of the picture window, I was looking for his car when it drove right past our house and down to our nearest Catholic neighbor.

"Hey, Holy Father! You missed us!" I cried, flying out of the chair and onto the front porch, but he did not notice me.

"Mommy, Mommy! He's missing our house. He's going to Marjorie's. Go down and make him come back."

My mother's troubled face showed weariness as she emerged from the kitchen, drying her hands on a cup towel.

"He cannot come to our house today, honey. He thinks Mommy has done something to make God angry."

"What, Mommy?" was my stunned question. My mother rarely spoke of God.

How could my mother make God angry? Yes, she attended church erratically, but she was kind and loving. She was beautiful and tender. I thought it was lies that made God angry, and not taking care of poor people, not being sorry when you pushed your sister down.

"You know, the things you tell Father Henry at the confession are a secret. I can't tell you now, honey. Please don't ask Mommy about it right now." Tears filled her eyes, but she brushed them quickly away as my father rushed into the room.

"Let's call Grandma Helen, Wabbit-Foot." He had called me this since my toddlerhood, when my mother stuffed the feet of my overall pajamas with tissue paper so that I would quit stepping on them and tripping myself. "Maybe she'd like to go get some ice cream with us this afternoon."

"Okay," I said, because I didn't know what else to say. I wanted to tell my mother about the penance I'd devised,

7

maybe get the priest down there right away, have him decide on something for her and bless our house anyway.

"Can Mommy and Jannie come too?" I asked. Something seemed suddenly broken there; I had a wish to repair it, a fear that somehow I'd caused the problem.

"I'll just stay here today, honey. I'm very tired, and Jannie is still down for her nap."

Time with Grandma Helen always seemed to do everyone good. My mother's mother, Grandma Finch, was the 'stay at home' grandma, and I visited her often, spending days baking pies, having tea, and working in her garden. But Grandma Helen, much younger than Grandma Finch, wore suits and business dresses because she had a job in an office downtown and for many years, lived in downtown as well.

For my weekend visits with her, she would ride the bus to our neighborhood to pick me up. After a brief visit with my parents, we'd board again and return to her studio apartment in the city, where she lived with my grandfather, who was a barber in a shop nearby.

Such outings made high drama for me, and I'd sit close beside her, watching her, and trying to match her demeanor and movements while the bus took us through the city. I would hold her hand and play with the rings on her fingers; her neatly manicured red nails, a source of fascination to me. I pictured them typing away on the important work I was sure she did as secretary. When we got to our stop, I would stride along with her, pretending to be wearing the same sensible but stylish pumps she wore, catching our reflections in the store windows of Yonkers Department Store.

"We're secretaries, aren't we, Grandma?"

"Oh, yes. And we've had a rough day. We need to go make some supper for Po. He'll be glad to have two pretty ladies to dine with."

Grandma Helen's city apartment contrasted starkly to my Grandma Finch's home, which was crowded with the paraphernalia of the floral and craft work of my artist grandfather, her brother crippled with polio, and her grown son, the ham radio operator, all of whom lived in her two-bedroom home.

My barber grandfather, however, was a cheerful housekeeper, and his working hours allowed him to dust, vacuum, and mop their small quarters. He cooked as often as Grandma Helen, but on the days I would stay with them, she and I usually made dinner. There was an economy in Grandma Helen's every move and activity, and I watched intently as she moved deftly from stove to cupboard to the tiny refrigerator of the efficient alcove kitchen, wiping and washing as she went, creating our dinner neatly, and making all traces of its preparation disappear when we had finished.

As night would fall, the lights of the city, the noise of the traffic on the street below, the music coming from the other apartments, confounded my sense of population.

"Does God know all these people in the city, Po?" I'd ask my grandfather.

"Yes, my dear. He's omnipotent and ubiquitous."

"He's what?"

I saw my grandmother smile and shake her head as she gathered up her sewing and turned on the radio.

"Let's just say, He's got a way of being around every corner," he chuckled. "Now, where's that book?"

9

"Help me say those words, Po."

"In your story book?"

"No, those God words."

"You want some big words to tell your Grandpa Finch next time you see him, don't you, little lady?"

"Yes. For when we watch Omnibus."

At 4 o'clock every Sunday afternoon, my Grandpa Finch tuned in to Omnibus, an Emmy Award winning arts and culture program sponsored by the Ford Foundation, which aired from 1952 to 1961.

My mother's father had been a scenic artist in the theatre in the Boston area until the stock market crashed. He moved his family back to his native, Iowa, and took up floral design to make a living. He never lost his love of art, literature, music, and philosophy, and he spoke with his grandchildren as if they would naturally have that same abiding interest, spoke with us as if we were little adults, never excluding us from the topic of the day.

Most of my cousins were too full of energy to sit still for Omnibus or the deep conversations that followed its airing, and my sisters were really too little. But I soaked it up along with my grandfather's stories of his brief stints dancing or acting on the productions for which he had created the scenery. My desire to be a Broadway nun likely had its birth in these stories.

Nevertheless, my barber grandfather, smelling fresh from a day of shaves, held me on his lap, more than happy to read to me or tell stories that I'd later repeat to my florist grandfather. The yellow parakeet, Petey Boy, would throw in his two cents worth, until it was time to cover his cage.

They kept a little cot with its own special quilts and blankets, which they pulled out of the closet for me, or my little sister, when it was her turn to visit. I felt adored there where that hum of the city gave me comfort, making me as happy there as I was in my Grandma Finch's garden.

Often my grandmother would let me play with her costume jewelry and her powder, perfume, and lipstick, the relished accouterments of the glamour I imagined in her working life. My grandmother's perfume was the solid kind, packaged in a blue plastic compact with elegant gold lettering. Sometimes I believe I catch a whiff of that fragrance here or there to this very day.

I would rub it on my wrists and dab the powder on my nose and write on the steno pad she kept at home for me. To be a secretary seemed a very fine and important occupation, and I pretended to be her, almost as much as I pretended to be a nun, or a Broadway dancer and singer.

Grandma Helen smoked, as did almost every adult in our family, except my mother's parents and her Nazarene brother and his wife, but she was the best smoker of them all, with a grace to her puffs that made me think of the few movie stars I'd seen. When my parents bought me those sugary, peppermint candy cigarettes with the red food coloring on the tips, it was her smoking I copied more than my mother's.

My grandmother would never buy them for me, though, and I could not know that Po was in his last decade of life suffering from tuberculosis. Nor could I know that lung cancer would claim her life before she turned sixty.

The afternoon of the priest's 'pass-by' was barely salvaged by my father taking me to Grandma Helen's home.

Father Talbert had already been to their apartment, and the palm frond was on the bookcase. I wished heartily that I had spent the night with them, and that God wasn't angry with my mother.

I told her about the parish priest not coming to our house. She looked at my father in an angry way, and then put her forehead down onto her open palm. I couldn't quite understand why she might be angry with him if it was my mother who had done something bad.

"God, Paul. What are you going to do?" she sighed. They both became aware of me, brightened, and tried to talk about something else. My father swung me up onto his shoulders and we went to the park, but it was quieter there than usual, and Po, not feeling well, had decided to stay at home too. We stopped for ice cream and took Grandma Helen back to her apartment. My mother was not there when we got home; a note said that she'd taken Janis with her to her mother's for a few hours.

After my father fixed himself a cup of coffee, he sat down on the davenport to read the paper. I was cutting out paper dolls when the telephone rang. My father answered it and took it into the bedroom and shut the door. He was still in there when my mother arrived.

"Hi, baby," my mother said, smiling at me as she came in the door. "What have you been doing?" she asked, as she sank into the rocking chair.

"Paper dolls."

"Where is Daddy?"

"On the phone."

I climbed up into her lap and caught the fragrance of her shampooed hair. "Let me comb your hair," I said, trying again to establish the loving routines between us. I jumped down to get the comb, and when I got back, she was sitting on the floor in front of the davenport, like always, so I could reach. She put her head back on my knees, and I pulled the comb through her brown curls and arranged them on my lap. Her beauty seemed infinite to me, and there was no one I wanted to be near more than her, as much as I loved my father and grandparents. My father came out of the bedroom and saw us.

"Two beauties in the beauty parlor?" he asked. Then, he looked surprised at himself that he'd said that. Mother did not say anything and closed her eyes, while I combed for a while. I thought of them jitterbugging or fox-trotting in the basement with their friends to songs about being in love. In the last months of my mother's pregnancy, their parties had ceased.

"All beautiful now!" I announced, looking around for my father to take up the chance to agree, but he'd gone to the backyard swings with Janis.

As we waited through the next weeks for the new baby to be born, I was getting tired of waiting for Jesus, but my timing was getting good on eating the reserved portion on my plate or in my bowl right before I received 'the look' from my mother.

My father was a distribution manager for the Des Moines Register and Tribune, and had to make routine trips around the state to encourage route managers. One of those times, he took me with him on a day trip to Waterloo. A cloudburst struck soon after we set out, and as the windshield wipers slung the water away, we listened to the radio. It played 'Stormy Weather,' and I sang along word for word, until I noticed the tears in my father's eyes. It had not occurred to me that the song might be sad. I liked songs for the melody or the feeling they gave me or because I'd watched my parents dance to them.

"Is that a sad song, Daddy?"

"Yeah, honey, but I can't believe you know all the words. You're one smart little girl."

"I like that other song too, the other tea song."

"Tea song?"

"Yes, you know, Daddy. Tender Leaf."

He began to laugh at my confusion between the popular ballad and the popular brand of tea, but I could still sense that something was wrong that I could not fix with my singing or cleverness.

In May, my sister, Susan, was born, and we were now three little girls; my father tacked a painted shingle under the numbers of our address that said 'Girls' Dormitory.' I thought that was a sign of his good humor and never wondered if he'd wished for a boy.

Soon after, however, I found myself staying with Grandma Helen again over a Saturday and Sunday night. She had taken the day off on a Monday, and took me home on the bus after lunch. When we got there, my mother and father were all dressed up, but Janis and six-week-old Susan were still at Grandma and Grandpa Finch's.

I was hoping Grandma Helen would stay for dinner, but my father took her with him as soon as we arrived and went to pick up the girls. My mother was wearing her best and my favorite of her outfits: a dark blue suit, her high platform heels, and the blue straw hat with big yellow roses on it.

14

"Mommy, you look so beautiful. Can I wear your hat when you take it off?"

"Maybe," she said, taking it off right then and sitting in the big overstuffed rocking chair. "Come here. Sit on my lap, I have something to tell you."

There was no fun secret about a trip to the park. Her hands weren't on her knees, her story-time eyes dancing. I climbed up on her lap and put my arms around her neck and leaned far back to see her face, but she captured me fast to her shoulder and said nothing for a minute. I rested my head against her blue suit, breathing in the luxury of her powder and her perfume. I wanted nothing more to happen.

"Daddy doesn't love us anymore, honey. He's going away to live with another lady."

The room, the shocked burgundy and chartreuse curtains with the art deco motif, the picture window, and the chair began to spin. I wanted her not to have said, 'Doesn't love us.' A mother wouldn't say that to a child, would she? But she didn't say 'doesn't love me,' she said 'doesn't love US.' In some ways, she was right, in some ways, she was wrong, but she said those words.

I tried to pull away to look at her, but she still held me tightly. She was crying now, and I began to cry too. "Is it because God is angry with you? Is it because I leave my toys in Daddy's way? Is it because of my dumb altar?"

"No, no, baby. I don't know why. He loves the other lady more than he loves me."

"Does she have children too?"

"Yes, three of them."

"Will they be my brothers and sisters?"

Startled, she held me out at arms' length. "They will never be your brothers and sisters!" she said. "And I will never share you or Daddy with anyone else. That's why Mommy and Daddy are getting a divorce."

A divorce. At six years old, I somehow knew about that word like I knew about the Second Coming of Christ. It was not a good word, perhaps a word that might make God angry. We both cried convulsively until we fell asleep in that favorite chair of ours and didn't wake up until we heard the jingling of the bells on the ice cream boy's bicycle. We went outside to wait for him.

All the neighborhood lawns were mowed and everything looked as orderly as it had that morning. She bought Fudgesicles for each of us and we sat there eating them on the front porch, mother still in her blue suit and high heels. I was getting down to the last part by the stick.

"Mommy, what would you do if Jesus came back to earth today?"

"Right now?"

"Yeah, right now."

"I'd buy him a Fudgesicle, sit him down here and ask him about a few things."

"Good idea, Mommy," I said and cleaned the last bit of ice cream off the stick.

Chapter Two
Queen of the Leaves

A person passing by the leafy slope, that November day in our neighborhood, would have had quite a start to see just the small circle of a child's face smiling out of a mound of slightly shifting leaves. But no one came past during the bright afternoon of my coronation. In the long days before television came to most American homes, children were sent outside daily to find whatever adventure or amusement they might: riding tricycles, zooming on swings, or the 'sky-scooters' of weather-bleached backyard gym-sets, digging in sandboxes, or pulling wagons full of dolls or baby brothers.

"Go blow the stink off!" Grandma Finch would say to bickering knot of cousins who had lost their imagination for indoor pastimes. And off we'd go, blocks away, to a grove of trees or down Miller Road to the pile of dirt beyond. We picked crab apples and ate them unwashed on the spot. We ate berries or sprigs of mint wherever we found them without ill effect.

So I'm sure my mother had no anxiety in sending a nearly five-year-old me out after lunch that day, in order that she and my toddler sister might have a quiet naptime without my restless pestering.

"Can't we get up now?"

"No, sweetie. We can't get up now, but you can. Off with you. Go play in the sunshine before the days get too cold. See if Marjorie is home. Come back for some cookies later."

What parent in a right mind could allow a child such relaxed ramblings in today's world full of speeding automobiles and lurking dangers?

But women, young and old, home all day, oversaw the quiet safety of our streets. The neighborhood children, who sometimes roved in groups, sometimes singly, were known by name and address, and any shenanigans were promptly scolded and reported to their parents.

My mother was right; soon deep Iowa snows would come, along with the heavy woolen leggings that would hang dripping in the backdoor hallway or over the hissing radiators of school coatrooms, their sodden scent marking the memory of winter.

Now, a heavy sweater and headscarf was sufficient bundling to get me out of the house, skipping down the street to the grove of oak and sycamore, to the embankment heaped with fallen leaves. I must have been about five at the time. How I have kept these sharp memories I cannot know, but they linger here into my advanced years, unchanged by time.

I viewed the bank, walked its slope, discovering a crunchy place to lie down and watch clouds move overhead. I said a few 'Hail Marys' as I had learned from Grandma Helen, and thought about the Queen of Heaven.

How graceful and lovely her images, how tenderly depicted, even in the dimensions of a stained glass window. I imagined her smiling at me.

In spite of the largeness of sky and earth, I felt in charge of the bank, the sun through the trees, even the leaves themselves. I went home, filled my headscarf with sand from the backyard sandbox, tying the colored square into a pillow, and returned to the bank. First clearing a my-sized space, I lay down and covered myself in the crisp and dusty leaves, scooping them around my head, elevated by the headscarf pillow.

Rather than naptime drowsiness, a kind of energized calm came over me. I saw myself from above, as if from heaven, but felt myself supported by the earth. I let my eyes and mind drift to everything around me, the birds, the fading grass, the clouds above, and the sun making patterns through the quaking leaves.

I was effortlessly and fearlessly letting myself blend into the scene I pictured. It was if I had been given a place card at the table of life, a seat from which to choose from its banquet. Having suffered no misfortune in life so far, I soaked up my oneness with the goodness I knew, the love of my family, my nascent understanding of God. I thought I felt, not only the love of God, but somehow being part of that love.

"I'm the Queen of the Leaves," I said out loud. No one contradicted me. I discovered that I could make proclamations for myself. I recognized that I could make some choices even as I lay there as a powerless child. I thought about being the good and loving queen of all I surveyed.

I cannot recall how long I lay in the leaves that day. But I know that I have found myself returning to that bank and the outpouring of love I sensed there when times of pain, sorrow or uncertainty have overwhelmed me. It will not surprise me if I find myself there in my heart in the hour I depart this earth.

On that day I learned to love silence as much as I loved music, to seek it in nature, a library, or a quiet room in times of turmoil and confusion. It was a lesson that would serve me well in the coming years.

Chapter Three
Train Case

My grandmother had guarded her sorrow with her goodbye gift: "A lady needs a train case when she goes on a big adventure."

So it was in a child's traveling box, bubble gum pink, I had packed the items of consequence in my nine-year-old life. My mother had filled one suitcase each of clothing for my two younger sisters and me. She left it to me to choose the items to fill the mirrored case I'd carry with me on the train to our new home; all our other belongings would be boxed and sent ahead for us.

To the expected cache of colored pencils, drawing book, ball and jacks, hairbrush, and barrettes, I added a strand of pink, pearlized plastic pop beads, the last in a chain of 'I'll be your best friend' presents from Nancy, my inseparable partner in neighborhood intrigues from the third to fifth grades, the gift Bible from the Foursquare Gospel Church with its comforting and colorful depiction of Christ surrounded by children, and a photograph of me in the garden corner of my fifth grade school room at Monroe Elementary with an inscription on the back that read, "I hope that you will always love wildflowers, Mary. Love, Miss Holt."

I also included an envelope containing a reference from my Girl Scout leader. Mrs. Reynolds had been complimentary. In her tidy handwriting, she'd fountain-penned, "Not a shirker, Mary Kay is dependable in carrying her share of team tasks. Her keen sense of humor and love of others make her a joy to be around. Her love of God, country, and family is unquestioned. She will be an asset to any troop she joins."

I wanted to believe my grandmother's prediction of an adventure, to let it cancel the way my chest hurt and the tightening behind my eyes I had when I thought of doing without her, Po, Grandma and Grandpa Finch, my friend Nancy, and Mrs. Reynolds.

In the crowded railroad coach, rocking along the tracks from Des Moines to Dallas, I pushed away the nausea of motion sickness and longing for my grandparents, examining again the items I'd chosen for the trip, reading again Mrs. Reynolds' words to remind me who I thought myself to be. I would soon become a new person: a new person in a neighborhood, a new person at a school, and a new person at a church. I had a new father.

My real father had made the deal: forgiveness of all the back child support in exchange for our adoption by the new husband. He'd resisted for months, but my mother, my step-father, and their lawyer, in a parry of telephone calls, letters, and conferences my sisters and I would know nothing about until years later, got him by the emotions, as well as the pocketbook, when they promised him a beautiful new life for three of us, my sisters and me: a brand new house, two married parents, a new start.

"How could you deny them the ease of acceptability of the same name as their mother?" their constant questioning ran. "Just sign and open the door of opportunity for your girls. Haven't they suffered enough, being known as the 'girls from the broken home,' while their mother has kept the bill collector from the door as you faltered in your financial responsibility? Aren't you being selfish in trying to keep any kind of ownership of them when you threw away your own respectability with this affair while your wife was pregnant with her third child? No, it's the least you could do for them, isn't it?"

Long before the old hash of 'if you love them, let them go,' they had persuaded him.

The night-long train ride made my sisters restless. Not quite four years old now, Susan was bewildered by the 'long, long ride' we'd been told about for weeks. She had napped fitfully all day and kept telling me she was not tired when I tried to sing her to sleep.

Janis had exhausted her six-year-old imagination on a package of drawing paper we'd been using to make pictures for our new father. We amused ourselves while our mother slept by balancing our way down the aisle to the water cooler at the end of the car and filling the flimsy cone-shaped cups with water, drinking the first round and refilling for a second helping to take back to our seats. My sisters made it back without spilling a drop, but the sight of fire shooting into the sky through the train windows sent my cup to the floor. I clamored back to my seat for a better look.

What appeared to be smoke stacks with leaping flames, filled me with terror. I awakened my mother.

"Mommy, there's fire out there!"

Startled, she pulled me to her lap for a moment. Gathering her senses, she looked as I pointed to the flames in the blackness.

"We must be in Oklahoma, honey," she said, soothing me. "Those fires are from the oil fields. They can't hurt you, and the fire from those pipes can't go anywhere but up into the air. Why don't you put your head down and sleep for a while. We'll get off this train in the morning."

I went back to my seat next to my baby sister, reclining it as far as it would go, and vowed not to look out into the night again.

My fear of fire began when a cigarette ash on a cotton throw-rug had sparked a small blaze in my bedroom, when I was four. No one knows who dropped the ash, but no real damage was done, for as soon as I screamed for my father to come save us, he was there stamping out the fire and leaving a blackened circle, the size of a dinner plate, on the white rug.

Part of my inability to go right to sleep at night stemmed from my need to watch for flames, and I often thought I saw them in the play of light through wind-tossed leaves, projected on a bedroom wall. My fear was further fueled by an autumn accident, when an ember from burning leaves settled on little Susan's sock, instantly melting nylon into skin, searing her screams of agony into my memory.

There on the train, I closed my eyes and pictured myself safely in the circle of children gathered around the Christ on the front of my Bible. "Good night, Jesus," I said out loud, and let the unrelenting motion put me to sleep.

Awakened by the slowing of the train at dawn, as we pulled into the old railway station in Dallas, I heard the woman behind my mother say, "You sure got some good girls there."

Already astir, Janis peered over the seat back. She had nurtured fantasies of Texas as the endless 'Spin and Marty' ranch we loved to watch on the Mickey Mouse Club. She had her heart set on a horse.

"We're getting a new house today. And a new Daddy," she crowed. Before the woman could respond, the train hissed to a stop and a flurry of activity broke out over the compartment, the smell of brewing coffee mingled with bathroom disinfectant.

"He's out there, he's out there!" my sister insisted, her hands pressed around her face to the window.

"Where?" our mother asked, leaning across the aisle as the jostling began.

"Right there, right there!" I picked him out of a small cluster of people standing on the platform, his arms folded solidly against his ribs, his mouth set in speculation. There, our new father stood, waiting for us.

He boarded the train to help us gather our things, and once we'd claimed our few pieces of luggage, Janis presented him with our drawings. He pretended a Texas accent while praising the work of 'little ladies from Iowa,' then took us for breakfast at the coffee shop before our drive home.

It felt good to be off the train, to have my old stomach back for a while before we got in the car again. Amid the morning clatter of cups and knives and forks, my sisters and I began our questions about our house and new neighborhood, Janis' face becoming somber, as she discovered we wouldn't be living at a dude ranch but in a new housing tract called Inglewood Park.

"What kind of trees in Inglewood Park?" she asked, remembering that Grandpa Finch would want to know. I hoped for the sycamore, oak, and cottonwood that we had climbed, raked up after, and loved in Iowa.

"No trees at all yet. We'll have to plant our own. Our own yard too, just like we want it." He tried to catch her downcast eyes, as he went on to describe our suburban frontier house.

"And Mary Kay will have her own room," he smiled. "And Jannie and Susie will get the big, big bedroom with lots of room for toys." My mother smiled too, and looked fresh and happy, in spite of having spent eighteen hours on a train with three girls in tow.

The late spring sun filtering through the window brightened her eyes as they sat together smoking the usual after meal cigarettes. Their smoke swirls twined together.

In the reflection of the window, we did, indeed, look like a family, intact and full of promise, but I had to shake my head at a little wave of revulsion that I hated myself for feeling toward my new father. Some people spoke of him as being handsome, but his dull green eyes seemed too deep set in his head, and I couldn't put away a textbook image of a Cro-Magnon man.

"So let's go find that new house, kids," he said, ushering us from the vinyl booth.

"What do you say, girls?" my mother asked.

"Thank you for breakfast," Susan offered.

"I love you, Daddy," I made myself say, willing it to be true. Janis said nothing.

An altogether new life was in fact what our new father had purchased for us in the suburban subdivision. Our buff-colored brick home was pristine and newly painted inside; every bit of furniture was new, bought directly from a model home. Such a home seemed enchanted to three girls who'd accepted garage sale furniture as fine and functional for so long.

As we wandered through the house, I could see how my old piano, which I'd paid for myself with US Saving Stamps, would be out of place in all this newness, but I missed its broken ivory keys and the release its playing offered me, its purpose, and its discipline. There would be no music teacher at my new school, no excitement of a lesson day when I could take my fifty cents tied into the corner of a handkerchief to a patient woman with a ticking metronome.

Our few boxes of clothing, toys, and possessions had arrived before us, and we found our clothes already hung in our closets and resting in the new 'Chester-drawers,' as Susan called them. I pictured this man unpacking and going though all our inventory of things. I wondered what he knew about me from my toys.

"You're too old to still be playing with dolls," he told me in a day or two, when I asked him to take my bride doll and Ginny doll down from the top shelf of my closet. *Hadn't he seen my room in our old house in Des Moines? Didn't he know that my whole social structure revolved around the culture of playing dolls with my friends?*

"Lots of girls play with dolls until they're fourteen," I volunteered. "I'm not even ten yet."

"Not girls who live in my house. It's time you started learning some responsibility and doing some work instead of playing all the time." He looked at me hard for a moment, but then he took the dolls and their box of accouterments from the shelf.

"One more summer. But out they go before sixth grade," he warned.

I clutched my silent companions, and believed he would forget his edict once he saw that I could keep my room clean and help around the house.

Children keep their intellectual and philosophical lives to themselves most of the time, probably because no one asks them the right questions or because their own questions cannot quite be framed. They're left to puzzle out fears and paradoxes on their own.

In the months after our transport to Texas, I remember pushing away surges of doubt and panic. I found no way to ask the rational questions: How had I come to this place? What had my role been in getting us here? How could I have consented to this painful displacement?

I would turn over in my mind, however, bits of history from the old life, perhaps feeling guilty for wanting less than what I then appeared to have.

I had sensed no poverty when we had lived in a rented two-bedroom cottage with a white picket fence on the back of a huge tree filled lot in Des Moines. The landlord had remodeled it from what had originally been the garage of a large home he had never found the money to build. My mother had hoped to buy the small house and lot herself eventually, and build her own grand house, like many of the others around it.

I was almost seven when we moved in, ready for third grade. We had left our decaying apartment house near the river, left the poor neighborhood with its deteriorating school that I nevertheless loved. There, I had relished my Bluebird troop, buying US Savings Stamps on Thursdays, and having a corporate crush on Mr. Hedburg, our young and handsome combined P.E. and Art teacher.

Leaving that apartment was easy enough, though. I had almost electrocuted myself, plugging in my record player one afternoon, and we stayed in bed, terrified to get up if we had to go to the bathroom at night, because of the 'water bugs,' my mother's careful euphemism for roaches.

When I wasn't imagining I saw flames at night, I perceived any shadows on my bed as large, glinting black darts, ready to storm my pillow. It had been a comfort that our baby-sitter, Mrs. Jenkins, whose daughter took us to the Foursquare Gospel Church downtown every Sunday and Wednesday night, could still care for us. The bus from her Victorian rooming house took her directly to our new house without a transfer. Mrs. Jenkins' grandchildren called her 'Mogie,' and we did as well. If we had been 'father poor,' we were certainly 'grandparent rich.'

My mother's enthusiasm for gaining her own land had lasted quite a while. She painted, she mowed, and she planted as if the house and lawn were her own. She saved her money from her clerical job. She learned to drive and bought her own second-hand car and got a better job at General Electric.

In the summer, we happily trouped out to 'ice cream suppers,' where she assumed we could have three of the four food groups for the cost of a strawberry cone or banana split. Two years of such scrimping had gained her little, however, and the winter after Susan's burn accident, she had taken to sleeping later and later on Saturday and Sunday mornings, leaving Janis and Susan in bed while I played in minor keys on my battered piano in the living room.

"That's nice, honey. Just keep playing for a while more so Mommy can sleep," she'd call when I asked if it was time for Janis and Susan to get up.

On the mornings that she came to pick us up for Sunday school, Mrs. Jenkins' daughter would sometimes find me braiding Susan's hair. She frowned with disapproval at my mother's closed bedroom door.

As I think back on it, my mother must have begun to sense that all her work barely kept her inches from welfare, rather than leading her toward any kind of independence.

Then came the afternoon of the big GE Christmas party. We met a man with a round, frightened child. She wore thick glasses magnifying a crossed eye. That party, Santa had terrified her, and I sat next to her holding her hand, while the man paid little attention to her and much to my mother. My mother, the romantic. Would she like to dance?

The day came when my mother would put the question of our future to us, looking for confirmation of what she wanted to hear.

"What do you think about Mommy getting married again, girls?" my mother had asked. Janis and Susan poked in their cereal bowls fishing for bananas among the Cheerios.

"OK, I guess," Janis mused. "We won't get any brothers, will we?"

"No. No brothers," she laughed, gently cradling Janis' face into a squishy-face and kissing it. I had not seen this much animation in her for a long time.

"Who will you marry, Mommy?" I asked.

"Why Duane, of course, Silly-Dilly. Who did you think?"

Duane. How attentive he'd been since Christmas. My mother loved to dance. So he took her to dances. Not always the big band dances she loved best, but country and western dances with men in sequin-spangled suits.

Sometimes we girls tagged along, legs aching with tiredness in the back of the car on the long, dark ride home, the three of us piled on one another. He brought her presents, brought us presents. She started getting up on Saturday and Sunday mornings again, taking us to our grandparents and not returning for us until late at night.

Who indeed. Who else was there to marry? Of course, it had to be Duane. I got a chill. I looked at my mother, suddenly radiant again, her pinched tiredness gone.

"Will you get to stay at home with us?"

"Well, if Mommy gets married again, we can move into a new house in a brand new place. We'll be just like all your other little friends' families."

"Will it make you happy?"

"It will make me very happy. But I won't get married again without you girls' permission."

We were three, five, and nine. *How could we say no? Why would we not want our hardworking mother to be happy?*

My sister's question about the brothers was one well taken. What had happened to the frightened little girl from the party? I knew that she was his daughter, but where had she gone? We had not seen her again after that afternoon.

"What about Patty, Mommy? Will she live with us?"

"Oh, poor Patty is gone to live with her grandmother in Chicago. Her mommy is very sick."

Now I too fished in the sweet, desultory sediment in the bottom of my cereal bowl. I couldn't think of the questions to ask to determine just what about marrying Duane would add to my mother's happiness or our own, for that matter.

Apart from a return of her zest for life, I couldn't imagine a better life for my sisters and me except that she could stay at home with us as she always said she wanted to do, making curtains, making our clothes, puttering in her garden. No more guilty joy for me when she had to stay home from work with a bad cold but would be waiting for us with hot chocolate when we returned from school on a cold afternoon.

My mother would entertain no more questions about poor Patty or her mother. None of us would know for another year or two that Patty's mother had been in a mental institution for a while, that there was indeed a brother farmed off to yet another wife's mother. Assuming our assent, she proceeded to charm Janis and Susan with talk of the pretty dresses she had in mind for the wedding, sweeping them away to a storybook ending, leaving me again with a store of questions I could not form.

What did it mean that we would be like all our 'other little friends' families?' True, we didn't have a Daddy, but except for that, there seemed to me no other lack. There were friends, there was music, and there was the garden of our grandparents' devotion.

The big gamble that a new father would restore a stay-at-home mother to us did not pay off. New houses and furniture were expensive, and within weeks of our arrival in Inglewood Park, our mother went back to work as a secretary. If she and Duane had any discussions about it, we girls were not included.

As she began sewing a new work wardrobe for herself, I wanted to ask her if she minded going back to work, if she was happy now that we had made the choice to leave Iowa and her parents behind. I longed for them, and missed my father too. We had no friends yet; I knew of no plans for swimming lessons or camp.

"I'm going to be lonesome if you go back to work," I ventured.

"Oh, honey. I'll miss you too, but you'll have Jannie and Susie to play with, and Duane will be home all day until I get home."

I hadn't occurred to me yet, that we would be at home with our new father day in and day out. He'd been going to work on the six to two-night shift at the aircraft plant in the past few weeks, but we had barely missed him as we cleaned up after dinner and settled in to bed early each night. His presence in the day seemed a part of summer vacation.

"When will we see Grandma and Grandpa again?" I suddenly blurted. "And when will we see our daddy?"

"Now, sweetheart, you have a new Daddy to see all the time. And I'm sure Grandma and Grandpa will come for a visit sometime next year."

33

"Don't forget, she has new grandparents too, Ruth. They'll be here in August."

There he was again, materializing in our private moment. She jumped just a little, and her fingers began working with the pins in the fabric.

"You girls expect a nice, new home in a nice neighborhood, but money doesn't grow on trees. You didn't think that your mother was going to stay at home all day long every day, did you?"

I looked at my mother, her eyes hidden in her handwork. We hadn't asked for all this, just for our mother to be happy and to have a father, who now seemed to be nothing like the fading memories of our own.

"No, sir," I lied.

"I just have to work for a little while until we really get our new family on its feet financially," she said as if in rehearsal. "Remember, school starts in a couple of months, and we'll all be busy."

She put an arm around me as I widened my eyes to stop any errant tears. Duane hated tears.

In the months after my mother returned to work, I kept looking for the romantic affection between my mother and Duane such as I'd witnessed long ago between her and my own father. No tousles of the hair, no touch on the cheek, no comments on her beauty or ours. No remnants remained of her recent courtship with Duane either; no dancing, no dinners out; we never had a baby-sitter. It seemed as if she were becoming one of us children, obedient and respectful, waiting in vain for a reward for good behavior.

A range of colors began to disappear in the orderliness of our new existence. Certainly some greens remained, at least through the spring and summer, as the new lawn we planted grew verdant from our watering and weeding. The muted hues of the fresh paint in our rooms, pinks and blues and rosy sandstone remained in my memories of the house.

But as if in exhalation or exsanguination, the colors of our past began to leave; my mother's once resonant face began to fade to monochrome. I know she must have continued to wear makeup, but the vibrant colors that had filled her cosmetic drawer in our old house, I could no longer associate with her face.

No one had gardens in Inglewood Park, at least no one we knew, for we visited no one's back yard. We grew hungry then, for the reds and oranges of our grandparents' home garden, the summer vegetables and fruit, the gathering of aunts and uncles for our garish and slapstick summer musicales, our grandfather showing us once again how to do the 'grapevine' he had danced in the real Vaudeville.

In my memory of Des Moines, there had been no gray; I could clearly recall the russet of rust budding on the yellow and blue metal lawn chairs, the diffident blue of the pesky jays in the cherry tree. Here, the colors drained to the turgid browns of the dusty and unoccupied school playground across the street, the not-yet-landscaped yards of our 'lazy' neighbors.

"No use in these girls sitting around with their crayons, when there are all those weeds to pull in the new lawn. Fresh air, sunshine, and some hard work are the ticket for them, isn't that right, Ruth?" he'd query.

"Out the door with you three," she'd say, shaking her head. "Come back in an hour for some pink lemonade. Go to the bathroom before you go out, though."

The door would close behind us, and if we tried the knob before an hour was up, we would find it locked.

For all my mother's love of romantic movies, love songs, and dancing, I never knew how she felt about sex until days before my own wedding. Having left all reproductive education up to that point to the Girl Scouts, she gave me this advice as I tried to show her the lingerie I'd bought for my honeymoon:

"When he's having his fun, just close your eyes and think of something pleasant."

Something pleasant. Something pleasant. What was she thinking of? I wanted to cry and laugh at the same time. Too reminiscent of that line, 'Think of England.'

Silenced by her revelation, I could only close the lovely tissue lined boxes and bury the hot contortion of my face on her shoulder. To laugh, to cry, or to scream were options we'd given over long before.

"Mom. You amaze me," was all I could say to her then. She'd kept this piece of her puzzle under the bed for years.

Our new father worked the night shift of engineers at the aircraft plant. He assumed his role as a taskmaster in the daytime, giving each of us daily household duties to perform, and perform to perfection. Even Susan had assigned chores, dusting the furniture that she was tall enough to reach and emptying the ashtrays. I was made their supervisor and given punishment along with them if their tasks did not meet his standards.

As if I were being groomed for a career in hotel housekeeping or a terrorist organization, I was to go after Janis and Susan inspecting their work. Janis' main chores were cleaning the bathroom and picking up after the dog in the backyard. I was to check her work and Susan's each day, and if I found any 'slipshod' work, I had to show them how to clean up the areas in question. When he appeared for his final inspection, we would all be in jeopardy of punishment if the work did not meet his standards.

"Toothpaste still on the back of the sink," he'd note on his clipboard. "Ten minutes in the corner for each of you."

At the end of his scrutiny, we'd get a tally of our errors, hoping for only time in the corner, his most benevolent form of discipline. Trashcans not emptied or a dirty toilet bowl could get us corporal punishment; usually a certain number of strokes with the belt or backhands to our faces.

I cannot look at a display of men's belts today without feeling the sting of his coldly-administered whippings, or wonder if the finely-tooled designs or braiding will leave their exact imprints on the tender backsides of little girls in the most respectable looking homes. Will they dress in the toilet stalls of their school gyms so no one will see the kind of artful bruises my stepfather inspected daily, to watch his handiwork fade?

When it came time for us to register for school, we were ready to fully assume our new identities. One evening after we had excitedly returned from the store with new notebooks, scissors, and colored pencils, Duane sat Janis and me down at the kitchen table, while our mother was giving Susan her bath before bedtime. I feared another long lecture, but this one was fairly simple.

"Here are the birth certificates we'll use to put you girls in school tomorrow. Do you see your names here?" he asked, pointing to the pink forms. We nodded our heads.

"That's your name now. That's your only name. These papers prove that you belong to me. Do you see that bastard's name anywhere on this page?"

"No, sir."

"That's right. Your father sold you to me, and there's no way to prove now that anybody but me is your father. We won't be using his name ever again, in this house or out of it. As far as your little school friends and your teacher know, all the family you have lives right here in this house."

"Yes, sir."

"Now, get ready for bed. Find your mother and give her a good night hug."

In bed that night, I thought about the lie that I'd been told and those pink forms. My own father's eyes came back to me, but other memories of him had become more and more dim.

I thought about his crew cut and the used cars he sold. I felt certain that my father could never have sold us, but there seemed no use arguing with this man.

Like hostages, my mother and her daughters were losing our identities to the captor. I began to make up myths constructed from snippets of our new father's history: It must have been his time on that ship in the war that had made him so stern; some evil of battle had crept into him and he just needed children to care for him to turn him back into the kind of father I remembered and wished this man to be.

All I wanted now was for this new family to work out, to be a beloved daughter of both a mother and father again. We could not know that the packages, cards, and letters our father sent were returned with the explanation that such intrusions of our past upset us so much that it would be unfair for him to continue.

Our new father had ways of testing our love for him. One Sunday afternoon, he snapped us with rubber bands, making little welts on our arms and legs. If we loved him, he told us, we wouldn't cry. I tried my best, but soon gave way to gasping tears. The snapping continued until I could 'be brave and stop crying,' which I finally did, so he would stop.

Our treat for going through the test was a long-awaited movie, but on the way, I vomited in the car, causing us to forego the pleasure we'd all been promised for a month.

The next test would be harder. With my mother looking on uncomfortably and smoking incessantly, he would have each of us hold our arms out to him while he brought the tip of his cigarette as close to our skin as he could, without actually burning us.

If I tried to catch her eyes during these sessions, searching for some note of anger or even some encouragement that she was on our side, it seemed that she had gone to some other dimension. I hoped that she was praying.

"If you trust me, you won't pull away and you won't cry, will you?" he'd said to us, face close to ours. I remember his mouth as he formed the words, his thin, almost-gray teeth, translucent and wavy like oyster shells.

It seemed that he brushed his teeth constantly, and he was always looking in our mouths for cavities.

We got fairly good at taking these 'tests,' and Janis, the most stoic, and bravest of us, became the best, holding out her hand without a twinge or a whimper.

"We're building real courage and discipline into these girls, Ruth," he'd reassure my mother. "They'll never betray us like that asshole father of theirs."

Somehow, he'd convinced her that what my sisters and I needed was tough discipline, after the coddling he felt our grandparents had given us since her divorce. Perhaps she was determined not to fail at a marriage again, just as we'd determined to be able to take a little physical pain without crying so that we could enjoy some happy family times.

Duane had labeled each of us with particular weaknesses and continually reminded us of them. Susan, almost four, was 'lazy and slow.' Her training punishment, when she didn't perform an errand or task quickly enough, was to run up and down the hallway fifty to one hundred times. When she would slow down, he would stand at one end and switch her little legs with a willow branch. When she'd 'done her laps,' she had to give him a hug and thank him for making her a good girl.

Janis, at six, had somehow been branded a liar, and he would quiz her constantly, teasing out nuances of truth in any statement that she made.

"Did you come home from school on time today?" he'd query.

"Yes."

"Yes, what?"

"Yes, sir."

"What time did you get home?"

"Four o'clock."

"No. It was three minutes past four o'clock."

"I thought it was four o'clock."

"No, you little liar. It was 4:03. Aren't they teaching you how to tell time in that damned school across the street?"

"Yes, sir."

"Then you just decided to lie to me, then?"

"No, sir."

"Come here. Let's see if you can take the belt without crying," he'd say to her. He'd take her into the bedroom and shut the door. Usually three 'licks' was a basic punishment for a lie, such as the one she'd told. I'd hear three sharp cracks, always administered to a bare behind, but no cries or tears, and the door would quickly open and I would hear him ask her for the hug due him to 'make us all happy again.'

Soon she could do this regularly, and got fewer times with the belt or switch than Susan or me. When he'd corner her into a 'lie' again, he'd put her in a chair in her room for hours instead of minutes, and not let her go outside to play with the dog, which was what she loved most.

By the end of our first school year in Texas, we were dutiful little automatons. Our mother witnessed very few of our punishments, as we always had to 'kiss and make up' with our disciplinarian before she came home from work. She always sat with us during the lengthy lectures he would give on weekend nights after dinner, interspersing his views of the world with the off-color or racist jokes, as if she too, were being indoctrinated by him.

Everything about school in Texas seemed foreign to the culture of Des Moines: no gardens in the classroom, no field trips to concerts and plays, no music in school except for singing. We had homework from school, something reserved for grades junior high and above where we had come from.

Our classmates teased our 'damned Yankee' accents out of us. By the time our cousins visited us the summer after my sixth-grade year, they thought we had Texas accents.

There were no newspapers, magazines, or encyclopedias to browse, and certainly no Omnibus, Girl Scouts, or afterschool activities for us because our parents' work schedules demanded that we be home to care for our little sister in the interim after Duane left for work and our mother returned home. We could not have friends over when our parents were not home, but had few friends anyway because we always had chores to do.

At eleven, I was still a round child, always predisposed to sweets, cakes, and cookies. One Sunday afternoon, my mother had made two chocolate pies for dinner, and I asked for a second piece.

"It's time to lose that baby fat, little glutton," Duane declared. Just as he'd had me smoke three cigarettes in succession a few weeks earlier, to discourage me from smoking, that afternoon, I was made to eat not only the second piece of pie, but also the entire second pie. This rich repast was followed by instruction on properly executed sit-ups, Air Force style. Fifty sit-ups. Twenty push-ups. Twenty leg-lifts. Three laps around the back yard. I lost the chocolate pie in the grass and my desire for dessert for several weeks.

Except for the chocolate pie, this was my daily regimen for the summer, and I began junior high in the fall no longer 'pleasingly plump' as my Grandma Finch chose to call me.

It was the next summer when I got my first period, and the season both my sisters had recurrent tonsillitis. I became proficient at taking temperatures and giving sponge baths and cough syrup. Those were the days when almost every child had a tonsillectomy. I'd had mine when I was four.

My parents decided that Janis and Susan would both have their tonsils out at the same time so that my mother would only have to be off work for one double recovery period. My sisters were actually excited about their trip to the hospital. Spending the night away from home for the first time since we'd moved to Texas and not having to do any chores for a week or so had them in high spirits. My mother was going to spend the night with them at the hospital after their operations.

The afternoon of the surgeries, my stepfather and I visited my mother and sisters. The little ones were unhappy and listless, the effects of the anesthetic wearing off and the searing sore throats beginning.

We didn't stay long, but went off for a movie, supposedly a treat for being left alone. We drove to a theater in a part of Dallas I'd never visited. A war picture was playing, horrible and frightening, with Japanese soldiers being attacked with flame-throwers, screaming and running and rolling, their bodies engulfed in flames. I covered my eyes as much as I could, but left the theater shaking from the cold of the unaccustomed air conditioning and the bloody and fiery violence.

He took me to dinner, but I could barely eat. I stared at the lines in his high forehead, and the tight waves in his thinning hair.

"It's time you understand about war. War is hell. Those shitty Japs ruined your mother's and my life with that war. Those guys got what they deserved."

I stared at my plate, but said nothing. I thought he was wrong, but I didn't know exactly why or how to tell him.

Instead, I said I didn't feel well and that I wanted to go home. He became uncharacteristically tender with me, holding my hand on the way to the car. When we got home, he offered to let me sleep in their bed with him. I said I wanted to read a while, but he insisted that if I didn't feel well, I'd better sleep with him.

My parents' bedroom was the only room in the house that was air-conditioned. The unit in the window made a steady rushing sound that shut out the night noises that usually soothed me to sleep.

I lay still and straight on my mother's side of the bed as he slid in beside me. He began to touch my breasts as he had many times before 'testing to see if they were ripe.' I turned over on my stomach, but he rolled me back over, moving my knees apart with the palms of his hands.

"Let me touch you right here," he said.

"No."

"Why not?"

"I think it's a sin."

"It's only a sin with someone who's not your father or your husband."

"But you're not my father or my husband. You're my mother's husband."

"No. I'm your father. Fathers must teach their little girls to be good wives, or they could end up frigid."

"What's frigid?" I'd heard him use the word before, sometimes in his off-color jokes.

"The kind of woman who doesn't know how to enjoy and love her husband. It's natural for fathers to teach their daughters about sex, they do it in other countries all the time."

"Then let's ask Mommy if we should."

"Your mother is an old-fashioned person, and so are your damned grandparents. I don't want to see that happen to you."

"I don't want you to touch me anymore."

"Come on, Baby. Just hold onto me like this."

He closed my hand around himself, and I closed my eyes as tightly as I could against my first startled sight of adult male anatomy, fighting back a rush of nausea.

"Our Father, who art in heaven, hallowed be thy name…" I started to pray silently to myself.

"Remember, girl," he said to me. "Your father sold you to me. I'm the one who's going to always protect you, the only one you can trust. You go out into the world, all alone, no money; the only way you'll eat is to be a whore."

"Please stop touching me now. I'm not a whore. I'm a good girl. I might be sloppy and forget things, but I'm a good girl."

"That's right. You just hold on tight to me. This is what you really want inside, to love your old dad and have him teach you how to love sex."

"It's wrong."

"No. That's why the world is so screwed up. They never let kids know about how good sex is."

Suddenly, he rolled away from me, moving and breathing in a way that frightened me, then he became still.

"You go to sleep now. The next lesson will be better."

"I should tell Mommy."

"You tell Mommy, it will kill her."

"Why?"

"She doesn't understand. You tell her, it might kill you too, or you'd end up in that shitty house in Des Moines again."

"It wasn't shitty."

He smacked me in the mouth. "Young ladies don't talk like that. And tell anyone about these lessons and you'll never see you mothers and sisters again."

He had silenced me. I turned over to cry in the pillow. I pulled it up over my ears until I could no longer hear the air conditioner. "What's right, God?" I asked and lay in the stillness, swallowing my sobs. No voice came to answer. I had to move the pillow to breathe, and when I did, I saw the bright dot of light from Duane's cigarette, the smoke wafting toward the air conditioner.

"Are you all right, girl?" he asked.

"Yes, sir." I replied.

"Go to sleep."

"May I sleep in my own bed now?"

"Yes. Go."

I opened the bedroom door to the wall of hot night air. I stepped down the hall to my lavender room, with the polished parquet floor and the frilly Priscilla curtains. I got into bed and wanted with all my heart for my stepfather not to be full of evil. I wanted to love him no matter how bad he was, but I wanted him never to touch me that way again. I thought about my own father and did not believe that he had sold me or that he didn't love me. I willed him to come with my grandparents to take us away, but I knew if he did not, that I must stay to love my mother and my sisters.

When I awoke to the hot sun in the morning, no rescue had been attempted, but the resolute remembrance of a reassuring dream insisted itself into my waking moments. I was certain I had been visited by the Christ in my sleep and given some kind of benediction for the future, that what I was experiencing in this time would not go on forever, that I could dream for a life and family somewhere out there that would be normal and safe.

What I had now was not normal or safe. A ribbon of light caught the pink of my train case on the top shelf of the open closet. I climbed the stepstool and pulled it down to find nothing left from my old journey but Mrs. Reed's letter enumerating my virtues. I lifted the envelope, read its contents once again, and placed it back on the bottom of the case.

After making my bed, I went to fix my bowl of cereal and thought of my sisters, safe in their hospital beds, my mother's soft hands on their flushed foreheads.

Chapter Four
Graven Images

"What's keeping Jesus?" became a question I would alternately abandon and reconsider for the rest of my life, as my parents' divorce propelled me from the elegant and European disciplines of Catholicism to the wider Protestant frontier, and finally to Eastern Orthodox Christianity.

Although I'd been surrounded by selected passages from the Bible before my marriage, the birth of our children and the immense responsibility they brought into our lives caused my husband, Jack, and me to give up our random consumption of religion; we became serious students of Biblical history and interpretation.

How would we instruct our children about God? Our parents' faith or lack of it, our own moments of encounter with the divine and evil demanded that we explore the boundaries of grace and what might have saved us up to that point. The Vietnam War and my beginning to coming to terms with what felt like my parents' betrayal, had forced us to question the role of God in our world and in our personal lives. Where were the lines between science and creation? *Was Jesus who he said he was or the biggest fraud ever perpetrated on mankind? Was the Bible literally or figurative true, or was it some of both?*

If there is one thing I continue to learn in this ongoing study, it is that there is something to be said for a child's sense of the immediate, and that there is the need to give up loyalty to a linear concept of time, if God and the Bible are to make sense. Prophecy and law are cyclical and layered in social, psychological, and spiritual perspective. The presence and love of God are outside of time, both immediate and historical.

When our son was three and a half, we thought we were preparing him well for the extended absence of his father on a six-month training deployment with the Marines.

We took him to the ship we had been telling him stories about; we showed him pictures of the places the ship would visit, read him poems about the wide, wide, ocean. We felt we didn't veil the truth from him when we'd repeat, "We will think Daddy has been gone a long, long, time when he finally comes home from the ship."

Every day after his father's departure, Bryan would ask me, "When is Daddy coming home?" and I would remind him that we had said it would be a long, long, time. In our daily prayers, he remembered his father 'far, far away over the sea.' Each day for over two weeks, I would try to reassure him with our mantra.

One day, he slapped his little bare foot on the linoleum floor and said, "It's been a long, long, time!"

There was nothing to do but scoop him up and cry with him in a shared loneliness for his father and a remembrance of my own childhood frustration at not being able to see the future clearly.

I sadly remembered all the times epistle and prophecy had seemed utterly incomprehensible and false to me too. Bryan's concept of time could not encompass six months, so he stopped asking after that.

Jack had made cassette tapes of Bryan's favorite storybooks before he left home, and sent more tapes along with the color funnies from Stars and Stripes, recording their ritual Sunday afternoon reading of the comics in his own voice.

"In the same exasperation, I'd likely had waiting for the Messiah as a child—" Bryan would often snap the off button of the tape player mid-sentence, and sit stone-faced for a few minutes before hurtling himself off the sofa to another activity, angry at this feeble evidence of his father's presence.

Post cards arrived, addressed individually to each child.

"Look, Bryan," his sister, Cadence, said one day when the mailman came, "A postcard from Dad in the Philippines."

"David and Goliath!" he yelled, ripping the card from her hand and looking at what he, ever the auditory learner, mistook for the Valley of Elah.

"No, you goose. That's the Philistines," the bossy big sister informed him.

It's so easy to be wrong when you're a kid.

We were living on the island of Oahu at the time, on the other side of the Koolau Mountains from Honolulu. There was a church near Pearl Harbor, not our church, with an immense neon cross and sign; its luminous lettering declared, 'Jesus Coming Soon.'

Define 'soon,' I thought to myself, as I drove past this landmark one evening, with my son's frustration over his dad's return in mind. I had been acquainted with such a sign in my own childhood.

The blue neon cross that rotated in the sky above the Foursquare Gospel Church near downtown, Des Moines, had white neon letters that spelled 'Jesus Saves.' In its sanctuary, one found no incense, no statuary, no richly robed nuns or priests, but its lofty green interior still profited from the glow of stained glass windows.

My first visit there had come a few months after my last visit to St. Theresa's convent, when I had a special goodbye breakfast with the nuns, and Mother Superior had taken me onto her lap to present me with a lifelike figurine of the Blessed Virgin.

"And here is someone who will always look after you, dear," she said. "She represents our love and the love of our Lord for you. We will miss you at St. Theresa's."

She pulled a small, white, square of handkerchief from her habit and quickly pressed her eyes. Clearly, she did not blame me or hold it against me for leaving the school. I thought I would see her each Sunday at church, but she knew otherwise.

She must have been concerned for my theological fate, but gave me no sense that I was in any kind of danger. I often return to the memory of the warm, bustling yet quiet convent kitchen, when I need a sense of love and peace. Unlike other Catholics I know, I experienced only firm discipline, mixed with a kind seriousness, never any kind of cruel reprimand in my years at St. Theresa.

My mother's anger at her excommunication and new status as single mother precluded her considering payment of tuition to school, run by the institution that now rejected her, although I now know my Grandmother Helen had offered to help.

After my mother moved me into public school, she made her feelings known about the hypocrisy of the Church, so that no Catholics ventured to take us with them to mass. There was still Bishop Sheen on television, but I felt certain I needed to be in the place where the rituals were performed.

I discovered that if I left home early enough, I could walk around the Stations of the Cross in the empty sanctuary at St. Theresa's, which was on my way to the new school.

At the hour I came by, mass was already over and classes had begun in the adjoining convent/classroom buildings; unfortunately, my detour sometimes made me late for public school. After a few notes home to that effect, our new babysitter, Mrs. Jenkins, would put Susan in the stroller and take Janis along, supposedly showing me how not to 'dawdle' on the way to school. I asked her one morning if we had time to do the Stations of the Cross.

"Oh, my no, dear. I wouldn't go in there where there's idol worship," she said.

Idols. When I thought of them, I pictured the huge golden calf from the Moses and the Ten Commandments book.

"There are no idols in there," I replied.

"There certainly are. Statues, graven images," was her stern remark. I hardly knew what to say. Without catechism class or visits to my Catholic grandparents, there seemed no place to ask questions about idols or graven images.

My mother had hired Mrs. Jenkins for her grandmotherly manner and appearance, her excellent references, and her willingness to be both housekeeper and nanny to three girls for a few dollars a week and bus fare.

Though I have many good memories of this loving woman, on that afternoon she tried to talk me out of my Blessed Virgin, explaining that keeping it by my bed was like worshipping idols. I resisted in the same way I would when she later tried to disabuse me of my belief in Santa Claus or the Easter Bunny.

I was a believer. Saints and symbols were innocent until completely proven guilty. One day, the figure of the Lord's Mother simply went missing.

It wasn't long before she'd arranged with my mother for someone from the Foursquare Gospel Church to pick up my sisters and me each Sunday morning and Wednesday evening.

There were no prayer books or missals in this place, but Bibles for everyone, and nice prizes for memorizing verses at Sunday school, some of which I already knew. Children progressed from the shortest verse in the Bible, 'Jesus wept,' to the Twenty Third and the One Hundredth Psalm, but it sometimes irritated me to hear their hurried, lifeless renderings.

Sister Miriam had taught us to read and memorize everything 'with feeling.' These folk saved their feeling for a kind of music I had not experienced in the Catholic Church: the singing of low-church hymns and children's songs with tunes that seemed alternately composed by Stephen Foster or John Philip Sousa, most in major keys.

These simple songs centered on Christ or God, the Father, some of them on the joys of heaven, with voices bolstered by a reverberating organ in the sanctuary on Sundays or on the piano downstairs on Wednesday nights and Sunday school.

Gone was song or talk of the Blessed Virgin or the saints. The rhymes of the hymns were easily memorized and drove our mother to distraction if I'd sing them in the car or at home.

"Enough of that now, sweetheart. Mommy needs some peace and quiet," she would say, pushing her fingers into her temples. Being a single mother of three could wear a woman out.

The women of the Foursquare Church, kind and plain, took a special interest in my sisters and me. They wore high lace collars on Sunday and housedresses on Wednesday nights, when they'd serve a big meal in the fellowship building across the street from the church.

From mothers and grandmothers who wore no jewelry but their wedding rings and only a little pressed powder on their pale faces, I learned the order of the books of the Bible, the difference between the Old and New Testaments, and heard Bible stories illustrated with cut-out fabric figures arranged on flannel boards. If children were quiet and attentive, such a teacher would let them place, move, or remove the characters or symbols from the boards. Being quiet and good continued to be my specialty.

Perhaps because I knew how to behave, perhaps because they were drawn by my need for affection and approval, or perhaps because they knew my story as a child from a 'broken home,' a cruel term I loathed, these women treated me with special care.

I did not know anyone at school or church, or in my neighborhood, whose parents were divorced. It always felt sad for me, but never quite shameful. Because even our father could leave us, I felt sure that it was the love of Christ 'down in their hearts' that we sang of every week that made them love me.

I tried looking into these people's eyes to see if I could really picture Jesus inside them, and hung onto my most precious thread of teaching from St. Theresa's: I could at least count on God to never stop loving people, no matter what they did.

My mother's oldest brother had joined his wife's denomination, the Church of the Nazarene, and they too, were more than ready to take me with them to Sunday school and church on the weekends we often spent with Grandma and Grandpa Finch.

The Nazarenes were an even plainer, more no-nonsense people than those at the Foursquare, although there was a special chapel and worship service just for children. Here, I found mostly white working people of good Mid-western stock, who used words like 'salvation,' 'righteousness,' and 'born again,' who laughed as heartily and often as the folk at Foursquare.

But there was not a whiff of incense in this church or even powder or perfume on the women, just the 'cleanliness is next to godliness' scent of bar soap. Here too, I could find a lap to sit on in 'big church,' which I often preferred to children's church because of the oil painting that filled the wall behind the dais at the front of the sanctuary: a luminous, life-size Christ, knocking at the door of a vine-covered cottage. I was starved for physical attention at the time, and no one could refuse a hug to a kid without a dad.

The common denominators of both these churches were the hymns and the 'altar call.' It turned out that an altar call would get me into serious trouble a few years later when we moved to Texas. At the end of such low-church services, after the hymns, the prayers, the scripture readings, the sometimes moving and emotional, sometimes dry as dust message of the preacher, the organist will begin to softly play the closing hymn. This hymn is closing, not only in the sense that it signals the close of the sermon and the nearing end of the service, but often seeks to bring closure to what the preacher is most often selling, the invitation to belief in Christ. In many churches, it is actually called the hymn of invitation.

Many a pastor would swing into the rhythm of his weekly entreaty,

> "And now won't you turn
> to the hymn of invitation,
> number 227, 'Just As I Am,'
> and with every head bowed
> and every eye closed as we sing,
> won't you examine
> your life this morning?
> Aren't you sick
> of the hopelessness
> of putting your trust
> in your paycheck,

your health,
your own good deeds?
Won't you come to Jesus now,
confessing your sin,
and trusting in the sacrifice
He made on Calvary
to save every last living one of us
who will humble himself
before the Cross?
Won't you come
and bow before Him here
and turn your life over to His loving care,
looking to the living Word of God
to guide your life?"

I have been to hundreds of such services, and there are many themes and variations of this litany. It sometimes goes on and on as the congregation may be asked to 'sing that last verse just one more time.'

The pastor was sure there was someone on the brink of giving themselves over to preposterous prospect that the death of one person could overcome the evil of all time past and time to come, that God could have become concentrated in one perfect human, that there could be a resurrection from the dead.

I believed it though. I would often make my way out of my seat and down to the low railing in front of the pulpit in response to the invitation. I didn't see why everyone in the house didn't come flooding to the front each time with me. *Didn't they believe this too? Isn't that why they were there?*

I had no parent to stop me, and it seemed no one had the heart to explain to me that once people made 'the good confession' that they were expected to stay in their seats unless for some sad reason they had 'backslidden' and needed to renew their faith.

According to the linguistic science of language acquisition, a child goes through a 'silent period,' where he or she listens and watches for verbal and non-verbal cues before beginning to speak. The three years between my mother's divorce and her re-marriage represented a similar period in my spiritual life.

By the time we were adopted and transported to the South, I had still not picked up on the idea that believers stayed in their seats during the invitation, that going to the front was a kind of 'one and done' experience.

The Inglewood Park Southern Baptist Church was waiting for me in our new neighborhood when my mother remarried and Duane adopted us. My mother was still as anti-church as ever, and our stepfather was alienated as well.

Mother and Duane had been married in a small ceremony in my grandparents' living room by the pastor of Duane's sister's church. My grandfather had done the flowers himself, and in the candlelight of the early evening gathering I watched my mother's smiles, her fair skin glowing. I felt happy that I too, had her dark blue eyes.

Almost immediately after the vows were taken, the pastor excused himself to another engagement, and when my new aunt left, Duane began to make fun of the man's shiny suit. My father had been a snappy dresser, and Duane too, took pride in appearances, always wearing cleanly tailored suits, slacks, sport coats, or his favorite colorful knit golf shirts on more casual occasions. He'd been in the Navy and the Air Force, and trusted in the value of well-pressed and well-maintained apparel.

Because their newly-wed need for a quiet Sunday morning had not occurred to me, it surprised me a bit in our new home that both, Duane and my mother, so cheerfully sent us off to the new church that was just the other side of the elementary school yard each Sunday.

My little sisters were not always enthusiastic about hurrying through their cereal and being put in scratchy dresses when there was a morning to be spent with our mother. But off we'd go to the friendly folks at IPBC, a sister clinging to each of my hands.

"So good to see you little girls again today!" was the greeting from the man perspiring in the early summer sun, dressed, nonetheless, in coat, white shirt, and tie.

"Always on time for Sunday school, aren't you? Good for you. Have we met your Mamma and Daddy yet?"

"No, sir."

Our parents reminded us often to say, "Yes, sir" and "No, sir" because now we were in Texas, and to always politely answer any questions anyone asked us. Good manners were very important here.

"You girls live around here?"

"Just over by Ben Milam School," Janis or I would say.

"Well, you girls go on and find your classrooms now. You know where that little one goes, right?"

"Yes, sir."

Janis and Susan would stay in the Sunday school area for most of the morning because there was a children's church service they liked to attend.

I felt entirely comfortable among the Baptists and liked their hymnal because it had many more interesting melodies and songs than my previous churches. The pastor was partial to long invitations and often preached emotional and persuasive sermons, but had few people come to the front in spite of repeating 'just that last verse' of the invitational over and over.

I soon felt compelled to prime the pump for him by going down myself. There was no altar rail at this church, however, and the penitents simply came and sat on the empty first row pew.

"Do you believe in Jesus as your savior, young lady?" a kindly elder would ask.

"Yes, sir."

"Will you pray this prayer with me, then?"

"Yes, sir," and he would pray the salvation prayer with his large hand on my head. Afterward, members of the congregation would file by and shake my hand. This was something new.

Something else new, was that after I kept doing this for a couple of Sundays, the preacher decided to pay a pastoral visit to our home. The doorbell rang one Sunday afternoon, and there was the thin-haired Reverend Jones, still in his suit, enjoying a cool moment in the shade of our breezy front porch.

"Why, good afternoon, sir. I believe you must be the father of these three, fine, little girls who have been coming to our church!"

"Yes. Hello," Duane said, opening the door to shake the man's hand.

"Stan Jones. Inglewood Baptist Church. May I come in a moment?"

"Well, yes. Come on in. Let me get Ruth to bring us some iced tea." He called my mother from the kitchen.

While my mother was introducing herself, I heard that genuine Texas accent from my room and hurried down the hall, wide eyed. No one from any evangelical church had ever come to our home back in Iowa, except to offer me a ride to church. Duane intercepted me and sent me back to my room, however, saying that I could come out later. He took Pastor Jones into the living room as I strained to hear bits of their conversation.

Pastor Jones was there to tell them the good news of my recurring decisions to follow Christ, and to ask them about my being baptized and joining their church.

"Mary Kay was baptized as a baby," I heard my mother say. "There's no need for her to be baptized again."

I caught only a few of the pastor's words, but they sounded a great deal like his morning message, something about how 'all have sinned and fallen short of the glory of God.' Perhaps he could convince them that the five of us should be there in the pews together, that 'the family that prays together, stays together.' Duane was having none of it.

"I don't need some god dammed hypocrite in my living room on a Sunday afternoon, telling me and my family how to live their life. I allow my girls to go to church anywhere they want to, but you'd better find some other suckers to fill the coffers of your church."

I could not stay in my room. My sisters, startled from their naps by the voices, joined me in the hallway in time to hear the pitcher of iced tea slosh on the living room floor and see Duane, fists full of suit lapels, hustling the speechless pastor backwards out the front door.

"Now, sir, I —" Pastor Jones tried to continue, but found himself staggering off the sidewalk onto the greenest front lawn of the neighborhood.

"Keep off my goddam grass," Duane said, almost sotto voce, but loud enough for the man to hear. We were all at the doorway by now and our mother's hands were shaking.

"Get in the living room, all of you," he commanded. He pulled some cleaning rags from a kitchen cupboard and threw them at me.

"Get that god dammed tea off the god dammed rug. You caused this mess. You clean it up."

My sisters were crying now, standing in front of the fan in the living room, giving their voices a strange vibration.

"Duane…" my mother began.

"Take the little ones to their room, Ruth. Get them quiet."

In a kind of stunned obedience, she was carrying Susan and leading Janis by the hand back down the hall. I began scooping the ice cubes into the plastic pitcher and pressing the towels into the rug. He watched me mop up the mess, his arms folded, silent, lips pressed together in a hard line. When I'd finished, I just stood there holding the pitcher and the towels.

"Did you ask that bastard to come to our house?"

"No."

"No, what?"

"No, sir."

"What the hell did he come here for?"

"I don't know."

"What did you tell him about us?"

"Nothing. That we lived by Ben Milam. I just prayed the salvation prayer after church a couple of times. They asked me if I wanted to be baptized, and I said yes."

"Then you didn't exactly tell him nothing, then."

"Um, I guess not. But that wasn't really about us, except that we lived by Ben Milam."

He did not appreciate my logic.

"Don't get smart with me, young lady. If you think you're such a holy little thing, then I'll give you something holy to do. For the next two weeks, unless you're eating or doing your chores around the house, you'll be in your room in the corner reading that goddamn Bible. If there's anything you don't understand, you can ask me about it, OK?"

"OK."

"What?"

"Yes, sir."

My mother was back in the living room now, and took the pitcher and towels from me.

"Did you tell anybody that Daddy and I just got married, honey?"

"No, ma'am."

She moved in front of the fan and pulled her handkerchief from her blouse to blot her pale, perspiring face.

"Come here, honey," she said, sitting in an overstuffed chair and taking me on her lap.

"You were baptized when you were a little baby. God doesn't need you to do anything else. You're a good girl."

"Don't coddle her, Ruth."

"I don't think she understood..."

"She understands now. Those Baptists are all a bunch of hypocrites, all they want is your money or to tell you what a sinner you are if you smoke. Get off your mother's lap, and put that extra kitchen chair in your room now."

"Yes, sir," I said, and went on wobbly legs to the kitchen.

"And don't bump into the damn wall going down the hall with the chair."

Again, I tried to hear the conversation in the living room, but could not. My mother had found someone to match her anger toward the church.

Not many of my new father's punishments would be so benign as his keeping me in the corner with the Scriptures, but this time marked the first punishment I'd ever received, for which I could find absolutely no blame, and could not see coming. His disconcerting behavior with the pastor left me unsettled and questioning.

"Duane seems a little hard on the girls," my Grandma Finch had said to my mother, when he had insisted on our helping her clean up the kitchen and the parlor after their brief wedding reception.

"Nothing wrong with a good disciplinarian," my mother had replied. "These girls can use some shaping up after three years with no father."

But this father was nothing like my fun-loving, polka-dot-wallpaper-in-the-basement father. While Duane often seemed generous with gifts and clothing for my mother or us, the cold, green eyes in his overhanging brow rarely smiled into mine.

I could picture no way of alerting either of my grandmothers to the scene in our living room. We were not allowed to use the telephone, and had no money or access to postage stamps. Our new world may have been more affluent, but far more sterile. There were no books, magazines, or newspapers in our house.

We had the run of our old neighborhood and visited the library and local shops every week in Des Moines, but nothing of the sort was within walking distance of our subdivision. There was no dabbling in our grandfather's messy oil paints or spending the afternoon at the art gallery with him.

Worst of all, I longed for someone to discuss big words with, to name the trees and plants, to tell me what a smart little girl I was.

I used my time in the corner to search my Bible for the verses I had memorized, and struggled my way through the King James English for some kind of message from God.

Only two verses away from a favorite old Foursquare memory verse, "Whosoever therefore shall humble himself as a little child, the same is greatest in the kingdom of heaven," I encountered, "But who so shall offend one of these little ones which believe in me, it were better for him that a millstone were hanged about his neck, and that he were drowned in the depth of the sea."

I'd wanted an at-home father for so long, and now the thought of drowning the one I'd been given, seemed defensible.

My neat theories of crime and punishment wrinkled under the weight of this injustice. I had not yet made friends with anger; sorrow had always quickly followed its rising in me. Loud conflict of any kind distressed me, and violence in any form revolted me, even the stomping of a bug, as I foolishly viewed any form of life anthropomorphically.

One of my favorite childhood books was a collection of poems and stories, the selection I remember best beginning, 'Hurt no living thing, no beetle nor a butterfly.' Now there I was, contemplating some kind of revenge or escape.

Two more weeks of Bible reading confused me, but also convinced me that if He came back, ending time as I knew it, I couldn't allow the gentle Jesus to find me plotting to desert my mother and sisters or even looking for a millstone suitable for my stepfather's neck.

Near the memory verse that said, "If it be possible, as much as lieth in you, live peaceably with all men," I was also startled to read, "Vengeance is mine, saith the Lord, I will repay." Better to let God take over the judgment for things I didn't understand. *Hadn't my mother said that I was good? Didn't she need me to be good, now that we were so far away from anyone who could help us if Duane became enraged again?*

Chapter Five
Model Home

The year I turned fifteen, a ready-made social life and religious community opened itself to me when a new family moved in across the street from us. Like our family, the Millers had three older kids and a 'late-life' baby boy they named Benny, now three years old like my brother, Nick. Chuck, Will, and Pam were all in the high school band with me, my one approved ticket out of the house. Best of all, most of my interaction with them could be done in person or the three-minute-limit phone calls Duane allowed me.

An egg timer sat by our one family phone in the hallway. Get a call; turn it over; when the sand is out, end the call. It was simple to spend a little time at their house and still be close enough to get home for household chores and to start dinner before my parents got home from work.

If it were not for band and music, I am not sure I could have survived the suffocation of my home, not sure I would have ever had a friend. The summer before junior high, the school district offered a band camp to give students the opportunity to learn a musical instrument and to boost the revenues of the local music companies.

Perhaps to make up for the loss of my piano, perhaps to create an image of the normalcy of our family, my parents purchased a brand new, chrome plated flute and allowed me to attend the summer band camp and continue music in junior high and high school. I was limited in the time that I could spend practicing my flute, as I was limited in time on homework, but it gave my life a forward momentum, a place to pour the energy of my mind and the overflow of my emotions.

"She plays like a gypsy," an early evaluator of my musicianship had written on a scoring sheet. This comment was not a positive one, as it referred to my lack of precise rhythm and phrasing, a hallmark of my self-tutelage.

Most students who continued in the band took private lessons to assist them in regional music competitions and later for scholarships and chairs in civic musical groups. My parents allowed me to participate in the occasional music contest as part of school music programs, but considered them unnecessary time and money expenditures.

If I were to enter any of these competitions, the fees would come from the money I earned from neighborhood babysitting, my other sanctioned ticket out of the house. They rarely attended concerts or performances at football games or other school activities. The appellation of gypsy satisfied me in some vague and piercingly romantic way, however, and I recorded the comment on the inside of one of my method books. I was a kind of gypsy moving from camp to camp, finding comfort at whatever warm fireside would welcome me.

Unlike Duane and my mother, Joanne and George Miller were the kind of parents who drove their children to distraction by complete involvement in their lives. George was an airline pilot and often had weekdays off to devote himself to community life. They were on hand for every concert, football half time, every softball game; there was no getting away from them. George was president of the PTA, an organization despised and decried by my stepfather as 'a bunch of social climbing hypocrites' but never to George's face, of course. There had never been another confrontation like the one with the Baptist minister.

Tagging along with this neighborhood family gave me an opportunity to experience and observe a functional, if not perfect family. Because I rode to school, band practice, and football games in Chuck's ragged blue Ford, and then to church with the whole family in their station-wagon on Sunday, Joanne and George treated me like one of their children, loved and praised, warned and looked out for.

By then I was the only one of my sisters who still went to church, and Methodism had become my current iteration of theology. I had progressed through the Baptist and Presbyterian forms of Calvinism, thanks to previous neighbors who had been willing to transport me back and forth to church. My new neighbors were a family who discussed the contradictions of their faith and held rigorous debate on the merits of the homily in the car after church and over Sunday dinner, most often at the airline employee cafeteria.

The open discussion of ideas including books, politics, and school by all members of the family was even better than a meal away from home, and I worked hard during each week to please my parents enough to allow me the privilege of the extra time with my 'adopted' family.

Unlike ours, their house was always a wreck.

"Hey, come on in!" George would cry to a troupe of adolescent society on his doorstep. "Let me move this pile of clean laundry," he'd say, and begin to adjust the stacks of newspapers, sewing, and PTA projects to make room for whatever number had appeared.

A swimming pool dominated their landscape-lacking back yard, where they hosted a YMCA home swimming program in the summers. Two dogs and two cats added to the ambiance and decor; a faint to not-so-faint litter box aroma sometimes combined with the essence of chlorine and wet towels to greet guests at the door. It was difficult to escape without taking home a little pet hair from whatever seat might have been found for you.

"I see you've been to that filthy sty again," Duane would say. "Keep going over there, you'll pick up some rotten disease."

I knew better than to reply or defend or comment to him: 'quibbling,' he called it. I wanted to tell him that there would be lots of people coming down with whatever could be picked up across the street, as laughing, talking people were welcomed at their home almost every day of the week, and what they might catch was nothing much more fearful than the joy of life. Chuck and Will and Pam's family represented what I imagined a 'normal' family would be: messy but loving. That's how my Grandma and Grandpa Finch's home had felt. Our house could not have been normal in spite of its gleaming floors and manicured lawn.

My mother had always declined Joanne's invitations for coffee or shared family barbecues, and I don't remember Duane and George Miller ever having anything more than a three-minute conversation. Such avoidance of the neighbors did not preclude the criticism of Chuck's parents so often part of my stepfather's dinnertime monologues:

"We mind our own business around here. There's more than enough to do taking care of our family without having to try to run everyone else's lives through the goddam PTA and tearing off to every ball game and concert, bullshitting about everybody's business in the stands."

Bullshitting. Goddamn. He saved that vocabulary for us. To an outsider, he appeared completely charming. He made his living representing electronic equipment firms and had a library of jokes, clean, slightly off-color, or downright filthy, ready to tailor for his audience. His public persona was impeccable, as were the environs of our home: manicured lawn, shiny washed cars, and a house that was cleaned top to bottom weekly by his daughters.

If anyone questioned, he could point to how pampered and spoiled we were with nice clothes, a lovely home, a dog, toys, even a shiny musical instrument. Sure, he and my mother smoked a couple of packs of cigarettes a day, but they rarely had a drink, and only went out to dinner once or twice a year. We were an upstanding, upwardly mobile American family. His job required him to travel, for a week or two at a time every other month or so. Our mother would relax then, and a peace would descend on our home that I could not bear to break by questioning her or complaining about Duane's behavior.

Childcare duties with the little boys, Benny and Nick, brought Pam and me together often, and although she was three years younger than I, we quickly developed an easy friendship.

71

Pam was bright. Too bright for most of her peers, probably too bright for me. She was straight A in math and chemistry and first chair French horn in the band. She loved word games, and we reaped the laughing scorn of her brothers and irritated our teachers and fellow students at school with puns and a game we called 'Word of the Week.'

Choosing some obscure or difficult word or phrase from the dictionary, Dickens, or Hawthorne, we would then use it in every conceivable, and often inconceivable, way in our conversations. We voted the archaic *invidious acrimony* from The House of Seven Gables, the top phrase of 1963. We feigned a corny sophistication by calling one other by our last names or last names of characters of the books we read.

We had a running disagreement over the merits of the Beatles: I thought their early work, their only work at the time, mindless and insipid. *Word of the Week: insipid.* She believed the Beatles were destined to be a musical bellwether of our time. *Word of the next Week: bellwether.* Of course, she was right, but I only came to appreciate their work after 'Norwegian Wood.'

Many hot summer evenings, we'd breathe in the honeysuckle and commiserate with one another as our little brothers crunched June bugs under the wheels of their tricycles, just before the street lights came on and we had to go in.

"DeFarge! (We were reading Tale of Two Cities) Why won't your parents let you take Spanish or Latin with me next year?" she'd query.

"Because, my dear Vengeance, they're grooming me to be a secretary. They say I'll need a good job when my husband divorces me. Got to get in those shorthand courses. I hate typing. I'm a horrible typist. But I'm going to a real college, darn it, with a music scholarship. Then I'll at least get to take Italian!"

She'd lend me her books and sometimes watch my brother so that I could get some extra homework done; there was a strict lights-out at my house at nine-thirty every night, whether the homework was done or not. 'Strict parents' were a common misery at the time, but mine were the unquestioned champions.

"Poor Mary Kay, her parents are so strict," Pam would complain to her parents or our friends, if there were something I wasn't allowed to do or somewhere I was not allowed to go. But strictness was generally viewed with approbation in our community; it was the parents who let their kids 'run wild' who were looked upon with disfavor. We girls never ran wild, and therefore drew no attention to our home situation.

Pam and I would scheme and plan and think of unorthodox careers for ourselves, but I knew I'd be lucky to get away to college because my parents were so set against it.

"Too much knowledge is useless," my mother would say. "You just need good job skills to fall back on. People with college educations are always upset about something, always going on some kind of crusade, mixed up in politics. Who needs it?"

In those days, there were only a few paths middle class women could expect to take: teach in public schools, do secretarial work, or marry and stay at home with the children, and certainly those were the limits of what my parents could envision for me. One thing I knew then, in spite of my childhood fascination with Grandma Helen's profession, was that I definitely didn't want that middle option. I could imagine Pam bored to death in all three. We knew there were women who where doctors, chemists, and politicians, but unfortunately, we didn't know any of them personally.

Within the first year she lived across the street from us, Pam graciously began to share her time with me with her oldest brother, Chuck. He was a painfully shy, brooding kid. I fancied him a combination of Heathcliff and Mr. Rochester with a nearsighted scowl. He was the complete math whiz-clarinet player with dark-rimmed coke-bottle-thick glasses and ever equipped with a slide rule and pocket protector. He smelled of the Brylcream that more or less tamed the cowlicks in his thick, dark hair. I grew to love that scent. And he was such a straight-arrow Eagle Scout and morally upright person that I trusted I had nothing to fear from him sexually. It took six months to develop a kissing-only relationship, which suited me perfectly. He generally ignored me when he was around his male friends, maintained a strict decorum around my parents, which I think irked Duane, who longed for a reason to criticize as well as belittle him.

It is eleven-thirty on a Saturday evening. The hi-fi has just dropped the last teetering platter from its chrome turret onto the five records already spinning on the turntable. Two Pete Fountain albums, one Al Hirt, one Glenn Miller, one Tommy Dorsey, and for the romantic conclusion, Robert Goulet. The 'at home dates' Chuck and I have are marked by the number of albums we can listen to before midnight when he must leave to return to his home across the street. I pride myself on being the perfect 'girl next door.'

Sweet, admiring, but with my limits: we hold hands; I recline with my head on his shoulder and his arm around mine. We look as long as we can into one another's eyes before we kiss, but an 'on the lips only' kiss. It's comfortable for me; it seems to be comfortable and safe for him too. Once he tries to explain why he doesn't try for more with me:

"It isn't that I don't want to. It's just that I'm scared I might not stop…"

"Shhh…" I say, putting my finger over his lips. "You don't have to explain to me. I'm not letting you get away with anything. Don't forget my parents are down the hall on the other side of the den."

I want to get his mind off that subject. I'd like him to tell me that he loves me and respects me so much that he'll wait forever for anything more than what we have, but even I understand that's just fantasy, just pure romance. I know his buddies and he have made oblique references to purported conquests, probably bragged falsely to one another. My aim is to get as much affection as I can while holding anything near to what my stepfather has tried with me as far from my mind as possible. I crave that old romance I witnessed years ago with my natural parents.

Goulet sings 'My Funny Valentine,' and I think: That's my Chuck. So shy and so homely, he's endearing.

Later in my senior year, he witnessed me being crowned the 'Band Sweetheart.' Walking me home after the banquet, he told me that he hadn't voted for me because he didn't want me to win and 'get the big head.'

75

A realization began to blossom that this boy had no idea who I really was, and perhaps didn't care to. Before Chuck and I were a couple and later after we broke up, he was mercilessly derisive of his sister and their little brother, Benny, tormented and tormenting because she was his intellectual equal and the only daughter, and Benny was the family darling.

"The only time I ever really liked my brother was when he was your boyfriend," Pam told me at a point later in our lives. But I liked having that civilizing effect on him, and perhaps that was another reason other than their charitable nature that George and Joanne so readily embraced me. In a kind of savior complex, I wanted to nurture the good qualities in him, for I did see a latent humility and sweetness in him that his outgoing, better-looking brother, Will, didn't seem to have. Mostly, he remained a safe and respectable love for me; we cost one another nothing.

In the meantime, Pam, Chuck, Will, and I, along with most of our band friends, were humorous misfits in the milieu of early '60s Texas high school culture when football was worshipped. If you were a guy, you were nothing if you weren't some part of the pigskin establishment unless you were in that next respectable echelon of basketball.

The female hierarchy was auxiliary to this hegemony, and the pecking order went like this: cheerleader, drill team leader, drill team member, girlfriend of football player, if none of the above; girlfriend and combination of any of the above were royalty. The rest of us were clearly peasant class. Our little group, except for Pam, rebelled against the music of the Beatles and had become big band era aficionados and connoisseurs of Dixieland jazz, with a little Peter, Paul, and Mary on the side.

We memorized all the words to the songs from Broadway musicals and sang them at the top of our lungs on the way home from band practice, hopelessly hokey. As miserable and lonely as we might have been individually, we found a satisfying camaraderie in our curious crust of society, and we reveled in our corporate non-conformity.

"Get pregnant and expect to never walk in this door again," I was warned repeatedly. "Not that all your spit-swapping with that impotent little creep will lead to anything," my stepfather always seemed pleased to point out. I, somehow, thought that the advent of a boyfriend in my life had diverted his attention from me. He never touched me now but contented himself with making comments about my hips or my breasts, sometimes complimentary, sometimes derogatory.

I watched intently to see if my sisters were the targets of more than the usual corporal or psychological abuse. He kept his advances on them so well hidden, and they so fearful, that it would be many years before I could comprehend how we, including our mother, were so cruelly deceived.

"You'll never have to worry that some guy loves you just for your looks," he'd remind me. "You've got nice tits, but you're homely as a barn door, broad as one too. Good thing I've taught you how to cook and clean."

Good thing, I thought. He didn't know that at that time I loved to cook and clean, that it brought me joy to create shine and order in the foul nest he ruled. I could practice caring for my future children in the daily care I gave my little brother. It was my job to get him ready for bed at night, read to him, and teach him to do his appointed 'chores' around the house such as emptying ashtrays and picking up his toys. I couldn't resent the time I spent with him; he was a sweet, uncomplaining child.

Get pregnant, smoke, or drink? Carouse with foul-mouthed guys in fast cars? I just wanted to go to the waffle shop after the football games with my nerdy friends. All I had to do was make sure that my mother had little more to do than make dinner a few times a week and usually he'd give me an hour or two after the game ended to be home. He'd listen to the game on the local radio station and note the time the fourth quarter ended. Exactly two hours later would be my curfew.

"You've got a watch, better pay attention," were his parting words, as I'd leave on a Friday afternoon in my band uniform.

"Yes, sir," I would say.

Pay attention to anything different than you, I would think.

Chapter Six
Background Music

I'm not one of those people able to write, think, or concentrate well on anything with music playing in the background. No serious writing in coffee shops or public places for me. It seems the only things I can do well while hearing music are dancing, cooking, or driving, and I'm not always sure about the cooking and driving, depending upon the music.

In my early marriage, it took me a while to convince my husband, who had known me since my undergraduate music major days, how listening to music and intimacy don't exist on the same continuum for me.

Music before: lovely, music after: divine. But I must pay attention to the music or the passion I share with and for him, unless I want either experience to be greatly diminished. So please no, especially no Bolero for me, darling. Not even a Puccini aria. The music compels my attention as I listen and wait for that next key modulation, for the crescendo or sostenuto. It simply transports me to another place, sometimes inside, sometimes outside the music. Part of the power of music is its ability, both to mark and transcend time.

A tourist near us at the USS Arizona Memorial had a cassette tape guide. Though it was 1979, my mother and I heard the music of the late 1930s and the Big Band Era as the tape narrated the events leading up to the bombing of Pearl Harbor. That was my mother's first visit to our family since my marriage ten years earlier. Although she had been divorced from Duane for almost six years, we had only short visits of a few days in Dallas with her when we'd come home on leave. None of those had allowed the two of us any time alone to talk, and she had never seen my home. Jack's assignment in the islands had offered us a refreshing change of scenery from our past life.

The mood was somber at the Memorial. The soft air, ambient with the scent of plumeria and tuberose from the leis of the visitors and those left at the memorial, offered a kind of consolation, as we contemplated the devastation of the attack. As we began to leave the site, my mother suddenly crumbled onto a bench nearby, sobbing, hands clenched at her forehead.

"Those damned Japs ruined my life," she cried.

I sat beside her, stunned at the dehumanizing word Japs, wondering if I had heard her correctly. Where had I heard that idea before?

"What, Mom?"

"The Japs. They started the war that took your dad away from me and made Duane crazy. If there had been no war, your father and I would still be married."

The scent of the flowers came in the wind again, and I felt dizzy. My mother had not mentioned my father for decades. I put an arm around her, my head on her shoulder. People passed by quietly, expecting scenes such as ours.

The man with the Big Band tape came by, and I wondered if the music had triggered these emotions.

"That's an incredible assumption, Mom," I said, trying to gather my wits, to catch her logic. The realization stunned me that she saw her own life so powerlessly connected in the historical struggle of two powers. A foreign face to portray a personal enemy. A world entity on whom to blame her deepest misfortune.

"You just don't know. We had our plans, our dreams. The war took them away," she told me, pulling herself up erectly on the bench, almost proudly, tears dispelling.

I tried to think of those dreams. She and my father would have been sixteen and seventeen before he left for the Army.

"What dreams, Mom? What did you want the most that could not happen once Daddy came home?" It was strange to call him Daddy. For years, that word could only have designated Duane.

"Well, we did have the house and of course, you girls," she said. "But we just didn't have the money that he had hoped to make. I didn't want him to take the risks he wanted to with his business, so he found other risks."

She rummaged in her purse for her cigarettes, found them, lit one.

"There's a lot that I've forgotten," she said and stood to walk towards the car, clearly wanting to leave that discussion behind.

On the way home, I thought of her divorce from Duane, how long it took her to accept that there was something deeply wrong with the way he treated her, my sisters, and Nick. How, when she would not brook my father's infidelity, she could let Duane live with Janis right in her own home, as if Janis were his wife? But then, I marvel at my own naïve belief, that I had somehow protected my sisters from his intrusions, although Susan had blessedly been spared much of the malignant attention he paid to her older sisters.

It was not until Janis made a suicide gesture and finally called Jack and me for help, that my mother began to come out of her hypnotic denial and decided that poor Duane was sick and that she must divorce him. But like the questions of old, these would not form themselves.

When we got to my home, my doorstep felt so safe, so entirely my own world that I could not spend any of those days we had together, opening wounds of the past. I wanted my children to have a happy time with their grandmother.

It took another twelve years, until a Christmas afternoon found my sisters and me alone with our mother and she finally broke down and asked us to forgive her for being so blind to all we had endured. She cried and cried, and told us she thought she had no choices; he made her believe she had no choices.

We asked her if she was afraid of him, if he ever hurt her physically. She told us no. If he had ever hit her, it might have caused her to flee, offered evidence that might have gotten him into trouble. But then she said that line again, "There's so much I just can't remember. How can you ever forgive me?"

"But we're fine now, Mom," we said. "We've made it through the fire, and we're trying to live the lives you would have wanted for us after all."

We never pressed her for more explanation, not wishing to bring her any more pain that had been inflicted on her and that she inflicted on herself. In our own private conversations, my sisters and I slowly came to see the careful, clever, and pathological way Duane had concealed the darkest of his abuses of us from each other, and from our mother.

The physical and psychological abuse he heaped on the three of us, and later on his own biological daughter when she came to live with us, reinforced the fear that we would, indeed, be separated from one another and from our mother if we breathed a word of his actions to any living person.

So, that afternoon, we impressed over and over on our mother our forgiveness. We told her she was our dear mother, and we would never stop loving her. We did not say, although we knew, that each of us will have to come to that forgiveness over and over, as we faced our own shortcomings and remembrances.

We seemed to have consoled her, and we all dried our tears before the husbands and children returned from their outing. I wondered if she could forgive herself and if it wasn't best that her memory stayed shadowed and selective. But the woman she was also remained a shadow I wished to uncover, and to rediscover the vibrant person I knew in my earliest childhood.

On her way home from a 'sentimental journey' trip to Des Moines, to visit her brother in 1999, my mother made a stop at my home on her way back to North Carolina. She had spent the better part of the week with her brother and a group of old friends she had not seen for over forty years, that he called together to surprise her.

I decided to use music to indirectly approach the buried truths I wanted to discover about my mother and father's life and love before and after my birth and those of my sisters.

Because she had often told me how much she enjoyed the feeling she got when we talked about the happy parts of her history, I used songs as anchors to catch and pull up any valuable relics from the wreckage of her life. I felt wise, but devious, in playing hypnotist with her in that way; we had long since passed those wrenching, tearful talks when she begged forgiveness.

With forgiveness behind us, I was now content to assemble the artifacts of our dark, ravaged, and now redeemed lives, waiting for an understanding that I'd accepted might never be fully realized.

My mother, in her seventies, still referred to the people she knew in high school as 'kids.'

"It seems like none of those kids have changed a bit," she told me, as she leafed through the North High yearbook for 1943 she carried with her, showing me their earnest faces, framed in hairdos I half expected to see on the next crop of college freshmen.

"Didn't some of these people come over and dance in our basement when I was a little kid, Mom? You guys danced to those old Glen Miller songs 'Moonlight Becomes You' and 'In the Mood' down there. And wasn't there an instrumental number called 'Celery Stalks at Midnight?'"

She laughed at the memory of that song and my vexing inability to stay in bed while they danced in the basement below.

"Never could get you to sleep when we put you to bed. We'd hear you calling to us through the heating registers to come back down because you weren't sleepy. Sometimes, we'd just find you sitting on the basement stairs, watching us in your nightgown."

"But all those songs were old ones, weren't they, from before the war? By the early fifties, weren't people listening to be-bop or the start of rock 'n roll?"

"We didn't care much about that stuff then. We just wanted to keep the big band era alive." She shut her eyes for an instant, pulling in the air, which became an extended sigh, and then another small laugh. I wanted to transform her into the wistfully attractive girl in the yearbook photos, the one on the swim team, in the glee club, so I poured us another cup of coffee and encouraged her talk.

In that session, there was much that she'd forgotten, chronologies she'd confused. I remembered that it was my stepfather, not my father, who liked Theresa Brewer, but rather than correcting her, I simply allowed my mother to reconstruct the minutia of her more youthful life, to try to know her as she was. She obliged me with lists of favorite movies she paid a dime to see, and the strange items she mailed to my father in overseas packages: photographs embedded in bars of soap.

I wanted to be careful to end our talks on a signal that said, "When I snap my fingers, you will only remember the things that will keep you safe and whole today." So, I tested my frighteningly uncanny memory of places and items from my childhood, by describing the improbable wallpaper my father put up in their party room: a metallic, silver background with huge polka dots of vibrant greens, yellows, reds, and blues.

"There was a little chrome fountain device too, that pumped whisky into shot glasses, wasn't there?" I asked, as I saw the memory roll over her face.

"My God. How can you remember all that? I threw away every photograph we had when I divorced your dad. No one remembers things like that from when they are five years old."

"Sure they do. I remember things from when I was two." And I proceeded to describe the interior of the house we lived in when I was born, to recall my grandfather making spaghetti on Saturday nights, and startling her with things I could not have been told or seen photographs of. I asked her question after question about her friends, about my father's job, about a certain skirt that she wore with giraffes on it.

Although my questions helped me make connections with my mother's younger life and sustain our friendship then, none of them helped me much to unearth any hidden truths of her psyche; she was giving up nothing. Talking like that I put myself under too. Perhaps she survived by forgetting, and I, by remembering.

I was in my bed, which was in a small room, right above the area of the basement that my father had made into their dance party room. They had often let me come down there for a short while before they tucked me in, and watched the black platters spin round and round. 'One o'clock Jump,' 'Sentimental Journey,' 'There Will Never Be Another You.' Glenn Miller, Rosemary Clooney, Sammy Kaye.

Along with the catechism of the church, I received a kind of catechism of romance from the moods and lyrics of their music. The couples drank and danced; they honored the custom of 'our song.'

Each couple got to lead off a dance that was their signature love song; I saw my father's hand, small compared to how tall he was, at my mother's waist, leading gracefully. She danced on her tiptoes, head back, looking up into his face, her red cardigan bringing out the red highlights in her brown hair. I saw them smiling, smiling.

For Ruth and Paul, the song was 'There Will Never Be Another You.' Now, the irony of the words almost embarrasses me.

I learned by heart the words to countless songs such as those, falling-in-love songs, being-in-love songs, unlucky-in-love songs, none of them reflecting the reality of trying to make a living after the war, trying to behave maturely after losing an adolescence to the necessities of mortal combat.

Not just the words, but the riffs, the harmonies of the original arrangements were intact in my memory as well, flavors that blended with my only emotional associations to the years before my birth: the deceptive impressions of the Judy Garland/Mickey Rooney, June Allison/Van Johnson romances. Singing and dancing all the way out of the war into the happily ever after.

Before my parents' divorce, I saw myself as a part of that romance, Ruth and Paul, the young lovers raising their babies in a 'My Blue Heaven' world, dancing in the basement with all their old friends. Although I would soon enough become disenchanted with Doris Day images of home and family, and grimly come to understand that love, romance, and sex are not the same, I could still connect with that pure spark of enjoyment floating aloft in the affection and music that I celebrated, spying from the basement stairs.

When my parents divorced, my mother got the record collection, and it moved around with us from place to place, the only remnant that would follow her through both marriages. In the lonely and bewildering days after the divorce, there were many hours to be filled while mother worked and father had vanished. I discovered in that library of records, not only entire albums of the big bands, but also other music that would ignite a new passion, the classical piano recordings of Arthur Rubenstein, Oscar Levant, and Jose Iturbi.

"She loves Paul's old records," my mother would tell her parents, "Too highbrow for me, but I guess if she likes them, we should hang onto them. Might be worth some money someday." My grandfather, champion of culture in a city he felt had no civic pride, insisted that she kept them.

"The child needs something to nurture her soul now," he would tell her, "Doesn't matter what they'll be worth in fifty years." He was right.

'The Ritual Fire Dance' transfixed me. Beethoven's 'Moonlight Sonata' put me in a reverie that had nothing to do with wartime romance; it was passion of a different sort: emotion, intellect, and stunning beauty.

I played Grieg's 'In the Hall of the Mountain King' over and over in the soporific afternoons after school, inventing dances about gnomes, treasures, and underground worlds. I gave up my aspirations for performing on Broadway as a nun, and considered pursuing the life of a concert pianist.

I disdained the small yellow disks that were my children's records. Bach's 'Flute Dance' performed perfunctorily in a rigidly peppy tempo held no charm. I wanted the luxury of full, orchestrated scores, anything Russian in minor keys. Such music gave the 'good happy girl' license to brood when I did not know how to grieve.

Here was quiet, free entertainment I could enjoy huddled on the floor with head down, arms around skirt-tented knees. The war time albums, which sometimes made my mother cry, and that newly discovered music were the few remainders of my father that could be kept alive without my mother's objection.

Sitting at my first Young People's Concert, I rolled the small globes of my faux-pearl necklace between my fingers until it almost broke and made my patent leather shoes stop bouncing on the floor, as the house lights went down. Even the boys had filed into the seats like gentlemen in their shirts and ties; no one had hit anyone in the bus. We'd been coached at school for weeks on recognizing the melodies of Sibelius' Finlandia, Beethoven's Fifth Symphony, and Tchaikovsky's First Piano Concerto in B-flat Minor.

I had taught myself to play its three repetitive opening chords and the right hand melody on a neighbor's piano. We had been reminded not to cough, to sit still, to watch the conductor carefully, and never applaud until he turned around to the audience, even if the music stopped.

But neither my father's records nor the teacher's reel-to-reel tape had made me ready for the Steinway's shattering of the nervous silence before the Tchaikovsky, the physical storm that broke over me with the Beethoven, or the inexplicable wall of emotion that crushed me with the great sighing opening chords of Finlandia. I could hardly walk back to the bus.

It had been two years since our father had left us, and I knew my mother could not afford a piano, but I begged her for one anyway, offering to help pay for it with my book of savings stamps. I hurt my best friend, Suzanne, by spending every afternoon I could at Amaryllis' house so that I could touch her piano and practice those three chords and melody when she would let me.

We looked in the paper every weekend for a bargain, but there were no ads for pianos for less than one hundred dollars. I had thirty-five dollars' worth of U.S. Savings Stamps, which I'd been pasting for two years from quarters and dimes that came from birthdays, the tooth fairy, or my small allowance.

Then, one afternoon, my grandfather Finch called to say that one of our distant relatives was moving and had an old piano they wanted to get rid of. They'd let us have it for the books of stamps. He used his old floral delivery truck and drove in the late afternoon Iowa sunlight, through fresh cut fields of alfalfa, to claim my prize.

There is substantive distinction for me between music with and without words, and even more, between music that one listens to or makes oneself.

The music of my earliest childhood was one with words in the foreground. Music without words, the orchestral and instrumental, nourished my inner life and the growth of my intellect as I grew older. Playing the piano, and later, the flute, would bring intellect and emotion together into the physical, the experiential beyond that of listening, into the existential and social.

Listening is physical, but only in a limited way. I needed to understand how the music was produced, even as I clumsily produced it; if I tried to do what I heard Rubenstein do, didn't that mean that I was part of some powerful class of people who could move the spirits of others? Performing later in a group brought more feelings of intimacy with others; for the length of the piece of music, I could feel myself literally in concert with my fellow musicians.

In those years that my sisters and I lived alone with my mother in her small house, the piano shaped my days and weeks: piano lesson day on Wednesday, practice each afternoon, Saturday morning serenades for my sleeping mother, impromptu recitals for anyone who'd sit down to listen.

Because he was so far behind with his child support, my father had limited visiting privileges, but on those infrequent Sunday afternoons when he and my grandmother, Helen, would come to share an hour our two with us, I would play for them and hear their praise that I longed for.

"This is the brightest, most entertaining nine-year-old in America," they'd say. Occasions for such performances would last for less than a year, for soon my mother would remarry and we would move seven hundred and fifty miles south, with as few of our possessions as possible. The piano would be left behind.

Like so many losses revealed to my husband long after the fact, the story of finding, then losing my piano had remained another of those bittersweet disclosures that would surface, who knows how, between two people who've known one another for years, in a languid conversation about something else, lazing on a quilt in the park.

"It was one of those monstrous, old, oak uprights, with ornate carving," I'd told him, "Some of it broken off from rough handling somewhere down the line. It had five missing, and three broken ivories. A piece of junk, really. I see how they couldn't justify the expense of moving it."

He was silent. Then, shaking his head, he looked at me as he had so many times when I offered up another long-forgotten memory. It was a look that said, "If you're ready, you can let a little more of that pain out."

"I just never knew you had a piano. Of course you would have. I should have known that about you." Some sad note was catching in his throat, and I was mystified.

"I wasn't going to be any better at playing the piano than I was the flute, Jack. I was in love with the music, with the idea of being a performer, but there were too few music lessons early enough, and not enough natural talent. I've long since let that go."

"Sometimes you let too much go," he said.

I wondered for a moment, if he was right, but as much as I believe in memory, I fear regret. While I would never choose it for myself, suffering that comes upon me from accident or injustice, even suffering I've brought on myself, has inevitably proved useful in some way.

My husband's identification with my loss, even so many years later, surprised me, endeared him to me, but that piano had given me what I needed at the time, it fed my spirit and filled my days with purpose. Wanting the piano, getting the piano, and later missing the piano, kept my mind off missing my father; one misery superseded the other.

Along with my father's records, my brief encounter with that instrument opened an astonishing realm of music for me: the hieroglyphics of music notation, appreciation of the skill necessary to translate notes to sound, the way I can now picture the sounds I hear in their written form.

I sometimes consider returning to the keyboard or the flute now that the days are long since gone when my stepfather only allowed me to practice for one hour a day, and replaced the time I would have rather spent on my homework or reading with child care and housework. Then, I think I have had too much good music in my ears to listen to myself practice.

Most of us could construct a playlist of popular music as a soundtrack for our personal histories and culture, then make a random choice from the list, placing ourselves with certain people, specific places, at certain junctures of our past. Music of the big band era puts me in two places: my earliest childhood, and its reprise in high school when my friends and I deviated from the norm in response to our ostracism by the sports obsessed strata of our small culture.

I was born in the vanguard of the baby boom, my father having barely returned from World War II when my mother conceived me. For them, it was 'the war.' Big band music sent them off to war and welcomed them home again. My generation's war became Vietnam, which had no musical send-offs or returns, only music of protest, denial, and bewilderment. My mother told me, as my friends began to be drafted and eventually killed, that every generation must have its war, and I needed to accept that.

I had barely begun to see how much she felt she must bear, and I did not welcome her proclamation any more than

I had been able, as a small child, to embrace as reasonable the nuclear threat requiring us to build bomb shelters or spend our classroom time preparing for attack. Or had I? Were we merely attempting to set ourselves apart from our popular peers, or were we in some way trying to step back into our parents' lives preparing ourselves for war by returning to their musical mindset?

Vietnam would be a war for which nothing could prepare us. The upbeat dance tunes of the '40s and 'I'll wait for you' romantic lyrics could not stand in the face of sixties 'free love' and the disillusionment of a war that would not be hidden from us by carefully edited movie newsreels.

Up to the point of that musical digression, and apart from my classical leanings, I had been a willing consumer of popular, primarily white music. Back in Iowa in the mid-fifties, we faithfully watched 'Your Hit Parade' with Snooky Lansen, and Giselle Mackenzie doing covers of top ten artists Patti Page, Perry Como, or Dean Martin, brought to us by our mentor, Lucky Strike cigarettes.

'L.S.M.F.T.—Lucky Strike Means Fine Tobacco' we'd mimic to one another. But there were other favorites as well from the radio: The Ink Spots, Nat King Cole, Eartha Kitt, those fascinating but somehow forbidden faces and moods I wanted to know.

I was too young to understand the screaming, swooning, and hair pulling of teenage women in response to the emerging icon, who was Elvis. But along with the Mouseketeers, he was a commodity for our emerging consumer group; as eight to ten-year-olds, we were also sold another brand of teenage romance.

Around the same time, my mother was beginning to see Duane, I collected 'Rock 'n Roll Pins' to wear on my bobby socks and got a hand-me-down poodle skirt from someone who worked at my mother's office. My mother likened the phenomenon of Elvis to the frenzy over Frank Sinatra, but there was something swarthy and humid that set him apart from the New York/Chicago sophistication of Sinatra, just as the South was different from the North.

While most of Elvis' music only amused me, there was something about him that frightened me too, moved me in a deeply melancholy way. There was a dark portent in his demeanor, as if something were moving in on me; something in his insistent sexuality reminded me of Duane.

In the years between my mother's marriages, two songs haunted me, a strange tune from the obscure Gogie Grant, 'The Wayward Wind,' and Elvis' pulsing 'Heartbreak Hotel.' I owned '45s of both these recordings, to which I gave significant airtime between the Rachmaninoff and the Mozart.

My mother entertained no talk or questions of our father, and even our few short Sunday afternoon visits kept him a mystery to me. When he would leave, I would fantasize about him in Grant's song.

Was he like the man who was born by the railroad tracks, where the sound of a train called him to the ways of a wanderer?

In backyard parodies of 'Show of Shows,' I could lip-sync Presley's song, emulating his angst, changing the words only slightly in my head to replace 'my baby' with 'my daddy.'

"What a little actress that one is," my Aunt Barbara would say to my grandfather.

In one of the last conversations I would have with my mother's father, he remembered the melodrama of that song and his chill of worry that a child so young could sing the blues so convincingly. He too, had hoped that a new daddy would fix that broken heart. He recounted the futility of trying to convince my mother to accept my father's attempt at reconciliation.

My interest in music and my ability to play the flute got me into college in the sixties. They weren't enough to keep me there. The scholarship I earned to Texas Tech University covered my small in-state tuition, but not room and board. My parents had told me that if I got a scholarship, they'd help me with my school expenses as long as I kept a part-time job during school.

The summer before college, I worked a full-time day job, took in ironing and did childcare in the evenings for a man with four children, whose mother had died of a brain aneurysm.

The money I saved got me through one semester, as room and board were still costly for me. When I talked to my parents at Thanksgiving about helping me with room and board for the spring, my stepfather told me there was no money in our family budget for that. They had just put on a room-addition and bought new furniture, including a small spinet for my youngest sister, Susan. She had a wonderful voice, and they thought she deserved as much music as I had been given. Didn't I?

"You've had your little foray into the sorority world. It's time for you to come home, get a respectable job and start contributing to your family after all these years of freeloading," Duane told me flatly. I looked at my mother, who would not look back at me, only to that smoke, ever drifting upward from their cigarettes. I could tell they were in inexorable debt again.

"But my grades are really good and I know I'm going to keep my scholarship. I want you to hear me play," I said, suddenly and foolishly feeling like the child in my grandfather's back yard calling to the adults, "See me, see me! Watch me play!"

"We'll have time for that later," she said. "You just need to understand that your Dad and I just can't afford a luxury for you right now."

I wanted her to at least acknowledge my hard work, but it was clear to me at that moment, that she valued only my complicity in keeping Duane mollified. She reminded me once more, that a college education was not necessary for a woman. There seemed little I could do.

"I'm going to see about getting a student loan," I told them. "I'm going to finish school."

Duane gave me a cynical smile as my mother squirmed in her chair.

"We'll see about that," he said. "I expect you'll be home after finals. I'll have a deal for you then."

Duane always had a deal. I went to the living room and put on Grieg's A Minor Piano Concerto and lay face down on the floor to listen to my soul.

Haven't I been patient enough? Haven't I worked hard? This can't be fair. I thought about all the people who wanted to go to school but could not, of all the injustices of history. I thought then about black women, scrubbing office floors so that their children could get an education, and my parents buying new cars and more furniture. I did not begrudge my sister her new piano; I wanted it for her, in fact, and I wanted that vague and ephemeral 'liberty and justice for all,' but had no idea what my role might be to bring it about.

For then, my role was to stay on the floor and listen to the music, let pain and anger roll over me and sense that my plight was a temporary one, that infinitely more horrible and unfair circumstances brought misery to others more and less righteous or longsuffering than me.

I let myself down into the mystery of grace, the remembrance of scripture: 'If God is for us, who can be against us? In my father's house are many mansions. I go to prepare a place for you. For now, we see in a glass darkly, but then face to face.'

Feeling this music no less sacred than the hymns of the church, I let it push me out into eternity and bring me back again, finding no tears for myself. A finer life of my own making would be possible in the dimension of human existence, and I believed another realm of God's making would be there for me when this one ended; I felt an inexorable link between the two that would require patience. I'd come this far; I could go on. I'd rely on goodness to prevail and endure the setbacks.

Upon return to Lubbock, I made appointments with all the officials at the university that I could. By the existing law, I was still a child and even unable to vote until age twenty-one; I'd just turned eighteen, my parents made far too much money for me to be considered a needy student.

A student loan was my only option, so I took the application process as far as I could. I was finally being immersed in the rich life of music I'd longed for and beginning to see a career for myself sharing music with children as lonely and confused as I had been.

How could I be derailed so soon in such a reasonable endeavor? Surely, there would be some rescue for me. Two days before the Christmas break, the Dean of Women called me into her office.

She was attractive and polished, her stylish Mary Quant pageboy shining brunette in the official light. She clasped her hands tightly together over the paperwork on her desk as if to pray.

"Your father will not agree to be a co-signer for your loan, Mary. We're so sorry, but you'll need to make arrangements to move out of the dormitory after finals in January."

"Yes, ma'am," I said. "Thank you." I wanted to say more to her, but there was no music to push the tears from my voice, and I would not cry in front of her. I willed myself out of the chair, out of her office, away from whatever consolation she might or might not have offered me in her elutriated West Texas accent.

The heavy resignation of the winter sky pressed its flat gust of refusal into my face as I jostled past other students through the heavy doors. Going down the steps of the building, I saw myself again from on high, one student of thousands, threading about a campus on the brown plains of the Panhandle.

The three hundred and fifty miles from Lubbock to Dallas waited for me. The canyons and arroyos, the cotton and oil fields would watch me going home for Christmas with my friends, and see me return again to finish my finals, only to make the final journey past them again in my stepfather's sedan, my ironing board wedged in the back seat, home to whatever 'deal' he had in mind for me.

It would be my next-to-last residency in my stepfather's house: His 'deal' was I would work from January of 1965 until August of 1966 and give him three-quarters of whatever salary I could earn as a kind of 'rent savings plan.' He would then pay me back with interest over the years it would take me to finish my degree; he would give me a student loan and a savings account rolled into one.

I would get 'free' room and board in exchange for cooking, housework, and childcare duties, share my mother's car for work and have limited use of it for my own pleasure with her permission. I fell naively into his plan because I had few other economic options, none of which I knew how to explore.

My mother seemed convinced of the genius of the scheme. "There isn't a safer or better way for a single girl to save her money, sweetheart. And you'll be helping us out of a tight spot now." She always made me feel that what we endured was some kind of favor to her. I had missed my sisters and my five-year-old brother, missed Pam, still in high school, missed the comfortable old Chuck, being near them again would be a consolation, and it seemed that my mother was genuinely glad to have me home.

One week after the end of finals, I was sharing a room with Susan, working in the circulation department of the Wall Street Journal, and making a budget for the quarter of my salary that I would keep. There would be clothing expenses for work, gas for my mother's car, and enough to hire myself a half-hour flute lesson every other week from the principle flutist of the Dallas Symphony to keep my music skills alive.

It was from this tall, too-pale man, whose studio was the anteroom of his stylish Highland Park home that I would come to understand my mediocre talent. He was to confirm what I had suspected: my previous small scholarship notwithstanding, I was no great performer.

"And who did you study with in high school?" he asked.

"No one, really. My band director helped me a little."

"I see. And you still received a scholarship to Texas Tech?"

"Yes. A tuition scholarship." It seemed suddenly quite small to me.

He sighed.

"Perhaps you should consider teaching music in elementary schools," he suggested, briskly and intently polishing his sterling silver Gemeinhardt with a soft cloth.

"Actually, sir, that's something I hope to do."

"And you believe taking lessons with me is necessary for that?"

"I think it's necessary for me to understand the discipline of music if I want to teach it in any meaningful way."

His brows moved upward, but he didn't turn his eyes to me. "Interesting little philosophy. You know, don't you, that I have many high school students waiting to study with me?"

"Yes, sir. I just need half an hour every other week. I want to try to get my scholarship back when I return to school in another year or so. I really want to continue my lessons with you."

He was now rubbing the lenses of his gold-rimmed glasses with the same white cotton cloth.

"We'll continue then, for another six months. If you don't progress sufficiently, I'll refer you to one of my senior students at SMU." He pressed his glasses to the bridge of his nose with an index finger. "Let's try the Bach and the Debussy for next time. Purchase the Vivaldi etude book by then, and we'll get down to brass tacks."

Having slipped briefly away from the authority and indoctrination of my home, I was determined to keep the path open to step back into that free, if difficult, realm I'd glimpsed in my semester away. I would often exasperate and sometimes, delight the maestro in the year he allowed me to continue study with him, but I cannot make myself recall his name to this day. I learned through my tutelage with him, however, to treasure my less-than-virtuoso students who nonetheless love studying their craft. It felt worth it to beg this man in order to keep my connection to the other music makers of the earth; creating melody seemed my only power, the only earthly gift I thought God had given me.

Chapter Seven
High Fidelity

My sample semester in Lubbock had been a powerful appetizer for me, a kind of glimpse of a promised land. Although I had to juggle a part-time job on campus and a full schedule of music rehearsals and study sessions, I felt amazingly free. There were thousands of students on campus, thousands of books in the library, hundreds of courses to choose from: a feast for my sheltered brain.

My parents had rarely allowed me to go to a slumber party, now it seemed dorm life provided endless such parties. So much laughing, so many silly shenanigans. I missed my brother and sisters, but apart from that, felt not one bit homesick. There was a great deal of tell-all about dates and drinking and a few allusions to sex in our late-night sessions in curlers and bunny slippers, but no one ever mentioned a stepfather who couldn't keep his hands to himself. I was sure that mine was some kind of fluke, some unmentionable mutation, and a tortured soul, who'd been tricked into some kind of Mephistopheles deal.

Cynthia and I, wing-mates in Knapp Hall, discovered one another as graduates of rival suburban high schools and fellow members of the marching band. She was instantly interested in me because I had gone to Irving High with her boyfriend, Jack. It turned out that in a high school of two thousand students, I had barely known the names of Jack Harkins and his younger sister, Gail, but I found Cynthia's personality compelling, and she found my instant adoration flattering.

Cynthia's interest in me gratified my need to find smart, well-read friends, once I had left home. She fascinated me with her confidence, her quick sardonic humor, her interest in politics, which had been another forbidden subject at our house. Sleek, thin, high-strung, she would lose five pounds during exams while the rest of us gained five. With shining black hair, green eyes, and thin, manicured fingers she looked, dressed, and moved a little like Audrey Hepburn on guarana.

Wanting her glamour and confidence to rub off on me, I found it easy to become her devotee. A big argument with her major professor, a significant misunderstanding with her mother, and I'd be there as the sympathetic ear, the right person to keep her ego buoyant.

Equally compelling was her relationship with this Jack who sent her flowers, wrote her frequently, and sang to her during the hours she talked to him on the downstairs payphone. She kept us updated on every twist and turn of their romance.

He had been extravagant as Chuck had been cheap. Jack took her to the Summer Musicals, to the finest restaurants in Dallas. Chuck invited me to swim in his backyard pool, to go Dutch treat at the Waffle House after the football games. He took me on double dates to dollar-a-carload drive-in movies, when his mother would make brown bags of popcorn and a thermos of lemonade in the summer or hot chocolate in the winter to send with us. Cynthia got flowers and dinners at white tablecloth restaurants.

Although she offered her sincere consolation when I had to leave school, my return to Irving after that fall semester seemed fortuitous to Cynthia. She found in me the perfect person to keep tabs on Jack, who had been working in a supermarket and playing semi-professional football back in the Dallas area. She saw me as no threat to their romance, as I was not yet completely disillusioned with my super-safe boy-next-door, Chuck. I'm fairly sure she saw me as the antithesis of her regal and charismatic personality, and I eagerly desired a link back to my life at Tech.

During the Christmas break before finals, she set up an evening for me to meet the celebrated Jack Harkins of Knapp Hall fame. We met at my house and went out for ice cream with Chuck, Jack, Cynthia, and his cousin Elaine, who had been her best friend in high school and attended Tech with us.

"She makes me laugh, Jack," Cynthia had said to him. "You should see her do her full imitation of Ado Annie from 'Oklahoma!'"

Jack lifted his dark brows at me for explanation. I'd been hearing about him all semester, but the intensity in his brown eyes startled me nonetheless. He was actually paying attention to me. I wasn't about to burst into song and dance right there at the Howard Johnson's, so I tried to dismiss the subject of my musical comedy expertise.

"I've just been trying to fulfill some childhood fantasies since I've been to college... tried out for the spring musical… didn't make it. Not that it matters, now that I won't be back," I told him.

"You could do some community theatre, couldn't you? There's a lot of theatre in Dallas," he suggested. "Who needs school to do what they really want to, anyway?"

His attitude about school was a little shocking to me, given what Cynthia had told me about him, but his idea intrigued me. Just as I opened my mouth to ask him where he thought I might try an audition, Cynthia put a finger to his chin, turning his face to hers.

"Well, honey, she's not an actress really, she's just a music major," Cynthia returned, feeding him a spoonful from her bowl. "Let's not talk about who's not going to school right now, OK?"

Elaine nudged me under the table and rolled her eyes at me. "Don't get her going on that," she announced to the whole table.

Cynthia was sure that Jack would try to get into to Texas A&M as soon as he took his GED and SATs. He had quit high school in the middle of his junior year, although he'd been an honor society candidate and president of the American Heritage Club. They had both been at the airport in November '63, when Kennedy had arrived in Dallas. There was a photo of them somewhere, pressed against the fence, with their welcoming signs.

Once I was back in Irving, Cynthia would send me things from Lubbock that she wanted him to pick up from me, and encouraged me to invite him on my outings with Chuck, ostensibly to keep him from being lonely.

Every other week or so he'd show up at our house and take my little brother and me out for a coke, and I would serve as a kind of courier for them. Cynthia was a risky and challenging prize for both of us, and we each had our loyalties to her. Those loyalties kept our discussions on an intellectual and fraternal level.

He would tell me stories of his childhood, helping his grandfather run the monstrous machinery of the drag-line at his great uncle's gravel pit, and how his grandfather had worked on half the highways in Arkansas and Texas. He was a serious student of Texas history, celebrating San Jacinto Day and commemorating the Siege of the Alamo every year. He'd worked hard, researching a paper on the Spanish Armada that his high school history teacher appropriated into her master's thesis, further alienating him from the educational establishment.

I discovered that he, too, had been shortchanged in the Southwest's obsession with football. Too short for basketball, but with a passion for speed and endurance activities, he loved track, tennis, and swimming, all of which held last priority in the resources of our high school's athletic department.

Male students were actually discouraged from those sports during football and basketball season. He played football anyway, in spite of the injuries a player of his size was bound to receive. Since his childhood, he had been full of energy, always running faster and farther than the other kids. His excessive drive and physical energy wasn't challenged by anything Irving had to offer.

School wasn't difficult enough for him. Other students wanted to pass, not parry ideas, so he found no willing partners for the political and philosophical debates he would invite in class. There were no physical challenges or adventures in our flat little suburb of Dallas, except for the dangers of risky driving and out-bluffing the local toughs.

Athletes and students with college potential were discouraged, if not outright forbidden, to take jobs after school. Boredom and frustration had taken its toll on Jack, and he dropped out of high school mid-junior year, an A student.

"There's something wrong with schools when they won't let you work and go to school at the same time, unless you don't plan to go to college," he'd complain to me. "They let my auto-shop buddies work half days, but tell them you want to go to law school or train for the Olympics, and you're stuck."

My little brother lived for Jack's visits. They'd wax his old '54 Ford together, put together the model planes Duane had never found the time to. My sisters teased me about how handsome he was.

"He's off limits, ladies. And remember, I have a boyfriend, Chuck."

"Eww. Mr. Slide Rule," they said.

Chuck didn't connect with Jack as many times as I tried to make him part of our visits, and was often moody and mute in the presence of Jack's spirited discussion of almost anything. There was only one level below a guy who'd played in the high school band, and that was the high school dropout. Chuck counted on his superiority in that way and had no intention of going into any branch of the service, hanging onto the safety of his school deferment.

Now that I was away from school, Jack provided another person with whom I could have a discussion on civil rights or the growing involvement of the United States in

Southeast Asia. I had hated my stepfather's racism and the obvious whiteness of our neighborhood.

Back in Des Moines, I had shared my school, Bluebird and Brownie Troops, with black girls, and missed their faces and friendship: Duane called me a 'little nigger lover.'

Jack's family had been solid Democrats for years. At that point, I was simply a questioner, groping to understand politics at all beyond the bland textbook definitions. By spring of 1965, we knew the war was broadening, escalating. Parents were getting nervous for their sons.

"I was watching a news special last night. I saw the Marines go back after the wounded guys. I think I should join the Marines before I let them draft me into the Army. I don't think I'd come back from the Army alive," he told me one afternoon.

"What will Cynthia say about that?" I asked.

"She won't get to say much of anything. I know I'm going to go one way or another. I can't stand the thought of going off to some college now, when every other poor working stiff like me is getting hauled off to war. Even guys with wives and kids. Our Dads took their turns, now we have to." He sounded like my mother there, for a second.

When he came to say goodbye to our family the day before he left for boot-camp, my brother cried and clung to his hand. Even Duane gave him an honest handshake and manly slap on the shoulder. His little sister would sleep on the floor outside his room that night, and I held on to him a little too long for just a friend.

Our friendship changed from one of intermittent personal visits to one of correspondence. He entertained my love of words by including small glossaries as keys to his letters, which included words like 'Charlie,' 'pogie,' 'hootch,' 'LZ,' and place names that were no longer classified. Sometimes, his commentary was telling.

"This is not the war my dad fought from his Coast Guard vessels; the enemy is in charge of the territory here. They know it inside out, know where to hide, how to trap you; this is somebody's home and not just some piece of land we're trying to get back for someone else," he wrote.

I joined that group of writers, careful to share news from home, without relaying unease and ambivalence beginning to grow in the culture. Those differences he wrote to us about were beginning to become vivid as we watched our televisions every evening.

It would take a while for the dissent of the coasts to move its way in to the middle of the country, just as the peace and love movement would have less influence on the ranchers, farmers, and oil engineers of Texas. Strong support for the war in this part of the country really represented more a support for Americans and the America we envisioned ourselves to be: people willing to put our troops on the line for freedom.

We needed him to know that there were still those who wanted him to stay safe, stay strong, and come back to us, even though we were beginning to question the meaning of freedom in political, moral, and sexual mores. So, I'd send him sports items from the paper and write about Marty's missing front teeth, or ask him if the top-40 was as weird to him as it was to me.

"What are they sending you to listen to over there?" I'd write. "Between Andy Williams 'Almost There,' Nancy Sinatra's 'These Boots Were Made for Walking,' the

Beatles' 'Hello Goodbye,' and the New Vaudeville Band's 'Winchester Cathedral,' you might get schizophrenic, if not psychedelic."

"We get it all over here, but I'll tell you one thing: I never want to hear 'Monday, Monday' again. Every time I hear it, I think of incoming," he'd write in reply.

I'd relate the details of my mundane life in the circulation department of the WSJ, and my attempts to hang out in the satellite newsroom, where I was clearly unwelcome.

That summer, during his training, he sent me his congratulations on my going back to school. Cynthia and I would be in the same dorm again, and I'd remain a link between them. His sister, Gail, was at school with us now too, and had become a part of the group who willingly revolved around Cynthia's exciting life.

The war provided a constant source of drama for her, and she kept a large green map of Southeast Asia on the wall of her room. Round-headed red pins marked the places of Jack's variously deduced whereabouts. She constantly annexed my letters in search of any slight mention of herself, as well as for research for her geographical and historical project on the war. The letters I received, filled with more information than romantic devotion, helped us sleuth out where we thought he'd been when he wrote them.

But romantic devotion in letters alone was wearing thin for Cynthia; being adored from afar was proving difficult for her. In spite of faithful letters and the gifts Jack had managed to send from the ports on the way to Vietnam, she was needing and finding plenty of romantic attention right there in Lubbock.

One of those cozy popcorn-smelling fall nights, on my way to her room with a letter I'd just gotten from Jack, I stopped at the huge hallway mirror in the corridor before her wing.

"How are things in Vogue?" I mugged at my face and form that would never make the cover of a '60s fashion magazine. I'd given up on old Chuck before leaving Irving again. My devotion to him and constant praise had given him the confidence to find another math major at Arlington State University where he was now, and lived in a dorm away from the surveillance of his parents. I was starting to have real dates with charming, but groping guys from my classes and the Tech marching band.

Striking a pouting pose, I took an inventory of assets: my good blue eyes, a nice small waist, and a generosity of curves that fell short of the skinny Twiggy/Hepburn ideal. My plain girl image was complete with no-nonsense wardrobe, an ordinary brownish-blonde Sound of Music haircut, and sensible shoes.

You're a B+, Queen of the Leaves, I thought to myself, *just like your grades.*

I dismissed the possibilities that I might rise into either 'A' bracket. It did not occur to me that there was any real brilliance or beauty there. Chuck never thought to tell me that I was bright or beautiful. My part-time job and hours of music rehearsals kept my study time in short supply; time and money for makeup and clothes were equally short.

I looked to Cynthia for study tips and strategies, and sometimes, a benevolent sorority girl would take me under her wing with a makeover from her cast-offs before a date. I remembered that Cynthia was keeping her scholarship, and hurried on to her room to borrow her notes on Richard III and to share my newest letter with her.

The door to her room was open, but I knocked anyway. She was putting on red lipstick, about to put a few lip prints on the back of a letter. The same imprints that had gotten Jack ten extra push-ups each in boot camp would now only bring envy in the hootches of Phu Bai. A wedge of sudden anger pushed inside me.

"Who's the lucky recipient of the Perfect Puckers this time?" I asked.

"Who do you think?"

"You're not still trying to make Harkins think that he's your one and only, are you?"

"Why shouldn't I?"

"Because he'll be disappointed to say the least when he gets home and finds out you've been spending your time at frat parties and on ski trips with Dave, that's why."

"It's for his own good to think he's got somebody special back here in Texas," Cynthia said, as Gail innocently entered the room.

"Sure. He's got me and this fine, upstanding citizen, Mary Kay here," she said.

"You and I both know he loves you, Cynthia. He thinks you're as good as engaged. Aren't you afraid he's beginning to suspect?"

"There's nothing in his letters to make me think..." her face began to pale, then redden. "I've read all your letters. He never..."

"Oh. You're so sure that you've read all my letters?"

"What did he write to you? What?"

"Nothing. Nothing yet. But if you don't say something soon, I think I ought to try to prepare him."

"You'll do nothing of the kind."

"Hide and watch."

"Well, if you want him killed, tell him. He'll get himself shot," she pouted.

"You flatter yourself. He's over there for more than you."

"Nobody knows why anybody's over there. I can't let him know yet."

"Not till you get a few more gifts, right?"

"You filthy little…" she almost whispered, and clutched the sleeve of my sweatshirt. Gail caught Cynthia's crimson fingernails before they met my face.

"You find a kind way to tell him or I will, I swear!" I told her on my way out of the room, as she collapsed, sobbing in Gail's arms.

I took the letter back to my room and sat, hands trembling, on the edge of my bed, dismayed that I'd damaged my most powerful friendship, likely beyond repair.

I opened the envelope and read again Jack's hopes that West Texas was still enjoying the crisp dry weather that he longed for in the relentless steaming vegetation he carried his pack and rifle through. He wanted to know that there were people going to school, making biscuits, sacking up groceries, just as he'd left them. What was the harm in Cynthia's deception? We sheltered him as much as we could from everything else, didn't we?

Jack's mother was at her desk at the Kroger grocery chain headquarters in Irving, when a government staff car pulled into her view of the parking lot from her office window. The department was decorated for the holidays, and it was the first year her son would not be home for Christmas. She watched the officer in his dress uniform get out of the car and start up the walkway. Closing the folder on her desk, she stayed in her chair. "My son cannot be dead," she said to herself. "My son cannot be dead."

A receptionist ushered the officer into her office and introduced himself, offering her the official document, informing her that her son had been wounded by sniper fire on December 19, 1966, his twentieth birthday. He assured her that the wounds were not serious and that her son was recovering, in fact, back in action after being treated by the field corpsmen. He declined her offer of a cup of coffee, and when he had excused himself to other duties, she closed her office door, prayed, and broke down in tears, the task left to her to tell her husband and family of Jack's wound.

In the next months, the job of sending officers to notify families of Marines who had been wounded, but not killed, would reach such proportions that the practice would have to be stopped. When Jack discovered that it was his mother who was notified, not his father, he changed his official paperwork so that she would never face that kind of bad news alone.

At a family gathering the next day, Jack's sister posed a question.

"Who gets to tell this to Cynthia?"

"I think you should, Gail. Or maybe Elaine," Inez would suggest.

"What about Mary Kay? Someone should tell Mary Kay, and she could tell Cynthia," Jack's thirteen-year-old sister added.

"Oh, bad idea, little sister," Gail replied. "You weren't there for the cat fight this semester."

Cynthia did react with theatrical anguish over the news of his first Purple Heart, but neither she nor I could find a good way to tell Jack that she was beginning to date around. I continued to write to him and receive letters with that peculiar moldy smell that made them seem still damp when I got them.

Sometimes, an insect would be immortalized between the pages as they'd been sealed to go out of the base-camp. He wrote about the 'scratch' he'd gotten from the sniper fire, and that when he'd written a letter half in jest to the Cracker Jack Company after opening a box and finding no prize, they had delivered a case of them to him via the US Mail.

He and his fellow 'grunts' began a letter writing campaign to Gillette and Colgate, praising their products, and found themselves supplied by mail with the personal care items that were so poorly and infrequently available through military supply chains. As miserable as the war had made him, he'd found a place to finally tap the stores of his physical stamina, his leadership qualities, and his devotion to his country.

By the summer of 1967, we'd tracked him from his landing for operations in Quang Tri Province, to Phu Bai, and the long offensive, when he fought his way up and down the Ko Bi Ton Than Valley, destroying and driving out Viet Cong and North Vietnamese Army regiments.

He'd made Corporal by February and trained as the communication chief for Mortar Platoon 3/26, leading a communications team during the move to secure the hills surrounding Khe Sahn and the defeat of the Ninth North Vietnamese Army in July.

By August, he'd made Sergeant and led his mortar platoon forward at Dong Ha, fighting two North Vietnamese Army regiments, who were attacking to stop South Vietnamese elections there. Not wanting to distress us with the terrors of combat, his letters reflected only the challenges of hygiene and the wonders of the country and tenacity of its people. What he wouldn't give for hot water, a good tube of toothpaste and clean sheets.

Now that I was on my own at school, I found myself a Presbyterian once again. Something about the music and a more formal nature of the service spoke to my Catholic roots. Symbol and order gave a sense of dignity to the worship. I was moving into a cynical period, the good work of the liberal arts forcing me to refine my beliefs and question every religious impulse I'd ever had.

Cruelties committed in the political incarnations of Christianity conflicted with my personal experience with His day-to-day followers. I wondered if I might be a better Jew than a Christian. For a while, I would only read the red letters of the Bible, deciding that I'd only believe the official words of Jesus. War and civil unrest often drove me to my knees, but could only trust silence as my prayer.

At other times, I would remember my dreams of the past, the moments when I'd felt Christ comfort the tormented child and, of course, my benediction below the branches that long, long ago autumn. I decided that I would keep going to church. I would keep on believing until there were no reason at all left to believe, until there was not a shred of kindness or self-sacrifice to be found.

Almost every Sunday, I'd find myself repeating to myself the scripture that recorded the bewildered follower saying to Jesus, "Lord, I believe. Help thou mine unbelief."

I prayed for Jack every day. I prayed for sense to return to the American public, to the government. I prayed for racism to end, for the war to end. No one seemed to be in control, very little seemed real. Faith certainly didn't clear things up, but it walked alongside my doubt.

While we were in summer school, Cynthia received a package from Vietnam containing two medals: Jack's Purple Hearts.

"These are my fraternity pins," he'd written. I think he'd begun to suspect that she was finding it difficult to be faithful, and the few letters I received from him made no mention of her. He'd asked only for prayers for safety and agonized over the deaths of his fellow Marines. Her friendship with me had remained, but tenuous. That he had now sent her his medals was too much for me.

"Send those to his mother, and tell him you don't deserve them." I told her. "Unless you really intend to marry him if he makes it home from there."

"I'd suggest you tend to your own poor little love life, girl," was her parting remark to me that day.

"I don't know if I could handle a man who loved me that much," I'd told my roommate later.

"What are you saying?" she replied. "There are no men left in Lubbock now, except for the agronomy majors. And they're in love with their horses."

I was in another of those Chuck type romances again, but was getting tired of guys who needed a mother or a sister along with romance. Could it be that I didn't know any men at school? They all seemed like boys. The current boyfriend, another music major, was working the summer in Glacier National Park and expecting homemade cookies every week along with the usual flattery. Corresponding with Jack, of course, was another matter; I tried to be the friend who listened to a man living every day with doubt, misery, danger, and death.

"Tell me more about your friend," I'd write. "Sounds like he was quite a character. I'm so sorry he's gone. Your grandmother sent a box of her famous little pocket pies to us here in the dorm, with a note that she'd send some to you. I hope yours arrived in better shape than ours, but they tasted great anyway. It's hard to believe that you're still getting boxes from home more quickly than ammo. You know, we pray for your safety every day and night."

That next autumn in Lubbock turned exceptionally cold, and the late October night was clear and still, as I walked up the broad sidewalk to the entrance of my dormitory, arms full of books, my little finger crooked around the handle of my flute case.

Tired from pushing myself and trying to stretch my tuition over as many units as possible, I pulled the heavy doors open, and could hear 'Lucy in the Sky with Diamonds' coming from somewhere down a hallway. I went to the desk to sign in and was met by a fellow member of the student office staff. She took the books out of my arms and put them on the desk.

"There's some kind of soldier in the formal lounge for you," she said, eyes wide.

"Soldier? I don't know any soldiers."

"Well, maybe he's not a soldier, but he's in a uniform and he's…"

"Oh, dear Lord. Is it a Marine?"

She opened the doors to the little-used parlor, and Jack rose to his feet. I still had my flute case in my hand.

"You want to play a little something for me now, or can I just tell you that I'm home?" he asked.

"You're home. You're alive. Thank God," I cried and ran to embrace him. My friend stepped back into the office and closed the doors. Even in 1967, public displays of affection in the dormitories were penalized. That night she was willing to be my lookout.

My tears covered his shoulder as I saw his chest full of ribbons. A black patch covered his right eye. I had known from a call from his sister that he'd been wounded again. His eye hadn't been badly damaged, but needed rest.

I held him at arm's length and studied the face I'd almost forgotten since we'd said goodbye before boot camp. He still looked young, his face full, his smile as engaging as the first time I saw him. But something about him seemed older as well, pain had left its traces on him.

"Are we OK in here? Can we sit down for a while?" he asked.

"Of course." I needed to sit down too; the room was beginning to turn around me.

"Have you seen Cynthia yet?" I asked.

"I didn't come to see Cynthia. She doesn't know I'm back. I came to see you."

"But—"

"Hush. Just let me hold onto you for a while."

"Gail said you're hurt. I see your eye, but are you OK?"

"We'll talk about that later."

A big difference between our fathers' war and our war was the quiet homecomings. They were usually small, family occasions, as the war and those who fought in it were becoming more and more of an embarrassment. Jack had left a year and a half before as a kind of hero, ready to defend the world against Communism.

By the time he returned with his three Purple Hearts, only the old guys met him with hearty handshakes and offered to buy him drinks. He got sidelong looks from longhaired young men. People pointed, and I heard a woman mutter 'killer' as we walked past her on a Dallas street, after he'd bought a ticket for me to fly there to spend more time with him.

We did see Cynthia on one of the two days he was in Lubbock. Gail had finally called her too, when I insisted that she see him. It was an awkward moment as she fingered the ribbons on his uniform and he pulled away from her, somber and formal. I felt somehow guilty for standing there, holding the hand of her former sweetheart, although I'd done nothing purposeful to separate them the last three years. She had been 'pinned' to a fraternity man for three months, but I could see she was chagrinned at his rebuff.

"And how are you now, Jack?" she'd asked him.

"I've had a gut full of suffering," he told her, his voice and eyes letting her know that she'd been part of it.

I realized, at that moment, that perhaps I knew Jack even better than she did. She may have read a few of the letters Jack had written to me, but she had made a point of publicly reading almost all of hers, and I knew the depth of feeling he'd expressed in them. Could or would that eloquent emotion, that devotion, now be directed to me?

The days I was able to spend with him on that return were strange and sweet. We would stay up and talk long into the night. With Cynthia no longer our common denominator or barrier, I could not keep from holding and kissing him.

"There is some kind of goodness in you, girl," he would tell me. "Some kind of goodness worth waiting for and fighting for."

"No more fighting, Jack. They won't send you back now, will they?"

"The Marine Corps needs me now. To fight or train troops to fight. I left a lot of buddies over there. I'm going to do what they need me to do."

My feelings for him frightened me. Someone loved me, but he still belonged to the war. I trusted him and felt a stirring for him, unlike anything I'd felt for Chuck, or Bill, or any of the other charming oafs who'd danced with me.

But clearly, he had not made a complete transition from the war zone to home; he was not himself yet. He was nervous and suspicious of sounds and shadows. His sister told me that he'd warned them not to touch him to wake him up, not to walk up behind him. What if the terrors of war had simply overcome him and he'd reached out for me just because I was the only one there? When he became acclimated to the US again, would he once again long for Cynthia, and she'd wake up and realize what she'd let go? Worst of all, would he go back to that God-awful war and be killed?

After he returned to his base in California, I wondered if our days in October had been some kind of '60s induced hallucination, that even those of us who shunned drugs and alcohol could have our minds altered. He wrote of leading a weapons platoon at Camp Pendleton, recovering fully from his wounds, running every day and getting stronger. I tried to resume writing in our old way, afraid of being hurt.

By his leave at Christmas time, he was more the Jack I remembered, still intense but calmer, laughing more. He was now more invested in staying a Marine and resisted any talk of getting out. He did not love the war, but loved his life of hard physical and mental training, and he still held an attachment for those left behind to fight.

He renewed our courtship with taking me to dinner and the theatre. He brought gifts for my brother, sisters, and me. We fell easily into one another's arms, but I still feared that Cynthia would come to her senses and fight to get him back. I still dream that she returns for him after all these years.

During the spring semester, we continued to write, and I made plans to spend the summer of 1968 at the same hotel in Glacier Park that my old boyfriend, Bill, had worked in previous summers. About a dozen Tech students spent the 'Summer of Love' as maids, bellboys, waiters, and dishwashers for whatever wages and tips we could save.

The Many Glacier Hotel hired a high percentage of music and theatre students because we were willing to provide free entertainment on our off-hours. My school funds always needed supplementing, so I'd opted out of summer school that year, and there was another chance to be in a Broadway musical that the hotel produced every summer.

I kept writing to Jack, but got few replies; a card or two without much news. I tried calling him on a payphone to a number I got from his sister, and the call was stilted and painful. I began to think that whatever had transpired between us was an aberration.

He knew how I felt about him returning to the war zone. He was an only son, wounded three times, so it must have been perfectly within regulations for him to be kept from the battlefront, but the Tet buildup required all the 27th Marines to be sent to South Vietnam. I'd assumed that his infrequent letters spelled a lessening of his interest in me. He let me think that he was busy with training exercises all that summer, and it was a good thing I didn't find out until thirty-two years later that he'd spent part of 1968 back in Ahn Loc.

I decided to stop writing to him, but he surprised me by asking to drive me home for Thanksgiving on his way home from Camp Pendleton. I said that I didn't think that was a good idea, and I didn't hear from him until Christmas when once again, he offered me a ride home to Irving.

Low on funds, I agreed to his picking me up before the holiday break. I had planned to tell him on the way home that I couldn't live with the prospect of his returning to the war and that even a friendship with him would be too painful. I had my speech all ready.

When his car pulled into the driveway of the rooming house where I was living, my resolve fell to tatters. When he hugged me hello, as corny as it still seems to me to this day, a voice in my head said, "Don't let this man get away."

A few days after Christmas, we lay on our backs in his parents' living room in the light of the tree.

"Do you want to hear what my soul sounds like?" I asked him. I'd brought home a vinyl recording of Chopin's E Minor Piano Concerto.

As I put the record on his parents' hi-fi, I told him I thought that if he listened carefully enough, he could be transported to eternity and back. After we sat there listening for a while, I told him what I'd told no one before: that Duane was not my father, that my parents had divorced when I was only six, and that I thought I could have borne my father's death more easily than thinking he didn't love me anymore. That was all I could bring myself to tell him then. He said nothing, but blotted my tears until they stopped.

When silence returned, we began a game we'd played for years and sometimes still play. It went something like this:

Jack: "What's the best piece of music you've ever heard?"

Me: "Live or recorded?"

Jack: "Live."

Me: "Sibelius' Finlandia. Des Moines, Iowa, 1955."

Jack: "Recorded, Dusty Springfield. 'You Don't Have to Say You Love Me.' Phu Bai, 1968."

Me: "I'm jealous of her."

Another round:

Me: "What's the best meal you ever ate?"

Jack: "At home or in a restaurant?"

Me: "In a restaurant."

Jack: "Youngblood's Fried Chicken, Irving, 1965."

Me: "You've got to be kidding."

Final round:

Me: "What do you want more than anything else in the whole world?"

Jack: "A son."

Me: "Then you ought to have one."

Jack: "But I'd need a wife, and I don't have a wife."

Me: "Well, you ought to have one."

Jack: "Are you available?"

Me: "Yes."

Jack: "Then we can tell our parents tomorrow."

I had not yet finished school, and a war was raging, but we began to swim for the rock of marriage against the tide of all that might seem against us in that turbulent time.

On Independence Day 1969, he wore his dress blues the day of our wedding, even though Dallas recorded a high temperature of one hundred and four degrees by noon. We planned the ceremony for ten in the morning so that the sixty people invited to the wedding would be able to attend the other holiday festivities that day and evening.

I had almost forgotten the old traditional rhyme about the bride's attire, 'Something borrowed. Something blue. Something old. Something new.' But after the rehearsal dinner the night before, Jack had offered me both 'something borrowed' and 'something blue.'

Tucked in the bodice of my dress that morning, was a red and blue Good Conduct ribbon that matched the one he wore on his uniform along with the Vietnam Service Medal and his three Purple Hearts. The red stripe down the sides of his blue trousers indicated his enlisted status in the Marines; three chevrons on the sleeve identified his rank as Sergeant.

The flower girl, who had known me all her life and thought of me as another child in the neighborhood, seemed impressed with his uniform and announced during the cake cutting, "Daddy! Mary Kay married a man!" Her remark brought laughter among the guests and reminded them how Jack's command voice had startled the quiet congregation during the recitation of the vows.

"Guess we know who'll wear the pants in this family," an uncle added.

"No. Guess which 'jarhead' is married for keeps?" was Jack's grinning reply, as he pointed a white-gloved finger to his own chest.

"Hear that, Duane?" Jack's father asked without fathoming the irony. "You're not getting her back!" I saw Duane's face go hard.

The photo of that instant shows me smiling, head down, a traditional blushing bride, with a bit of the Twenty-Third Psalm running through my head, *Thou preparest a table for me in the presence of mine enemies.*

I had only one regret on my wedding day; the secret cause of tears that began to well in my eyes as I waited for the opening chords of the processional: Duane would escort me down the aisle and give away what was not his to give.

"Stop your sniveling. You look ridiculous," he had said to me before he walked me down the aisle. "Just stick out those boobs and make your mother proud."

I wanted to grind my heel on his foot and march on alone, but I caught sight of Jack's square jaw and shoulders already at the altar. Though he is not a tall man, his presence overwhelmed the scene at the front of the church. This was his day too.

Instead, I spoke silently into my past, "I'm getting married, Daddy," not to Duane but to my own father, wherever he was. I put my head up and stepped ahead, continuing to pretend Duane was my father. I would protect my mother's pride, at least for another year or two. The greeting smiles of my husband's family coaxed out my own and cancelled the tears.

Chapter Eight
Near Fatality

I suppose the reason my husband's first girlfriend makes a periodic haunting of my dreams, is that Cynthia represented dangerous challenge for Jack, and I, the warm, calm waters of home. In some ways, the Marine Corps took her place, a mistress to his need for adventure and risk.

Heeding the caprice of foreign policy or the volatility of despots in the world, that mistress could pluck him away from me at any time. In fact, his preparations for her clarion call often demand the first allegiance of his time. It was me to whom he always returned, however, and I had the power of a safe harbor, a strong command post, and of course, his word of honor.

In spite of my love and trust for him, and the strong foundation that five years of friendship and correspondence gave us, we took a big risk in marrying one another when we hadn't spent more than two weeks in a row in the same town after we fell in love. We'd never been grocery shopping or to a movie together, although we'd spent four days of his re-enlistment leave on a trip to New Orleans. We'd never cooked one another a meal, and only seriously disagreed over one thing: his return to Vietnam.

Disagreement was still our weak suit. Either of us might begin a dialogue that followed this pattern:

"What's the matter?"

"Nothing."

"Are you disappointed about something?"

"No."

"Did I say something to upset you?"

"No."

We lie on the edges of our bed, ignoring the admonition: 'Let not the sun go down on your anger.' In our case, it seemed we never let the sun come back up on our exasperation. It usually vanished in the night as we thought things over separately and decided there was nothing really worth having strong words over. Sleep on your wrath and it will go away. Usually. Neither his parents nor mine had modeled conflict resolution for us, simply conflict avoidance.

It was a good thing Jack Harkins did not die in the early years of our marriage because it would be fair to say that, for a time, it was he that I worshipped above God.

By the time our children arrived, however, I understood that though Jack had given me a new life, and brought me endless pleasure, he could not be my God. He could not read my mind, was not infallible in his judgments, and I had mostly gotten over the naive misconception that we would never disappoint one another.

The closest I ever came to having an affair was the year our daughter was ten and her brother was six. July of 1980 had brought the four of us from a three and a half year tour at Kaneohe Marine Corps Air Station on the windward side of Oahu, back to our beloved home city, San Diego.

Cadence had learned to snorkel, boogie board, perform traditional Hawaiian dance, climb waterfalls, and hike the Koolaus. Her mother had been her Brownie and Girl Scout leader. Her days had been warm, barefoot, scented with the Plumeria blossoms that covered the tree by our front door; she and her brother had roamed freely on the dunes and playgrounds surrounding the officers' quarters at the air station.

Except for Hawaiian culture, she'd been able to transfer her life of Barbies, outdoor adventures, and softball with her to a new home, a new school, and a new church. For Cadence and her father, the basic fabric of their lives remained the same; their life work simply moved from one pleasant location to another, their support systems intact.

For Bryan and me, more difficult changes were required. Because we had decided to buy our own home upon our return to San Diego, I had returned to work. Never as adaptable as Cadence, Bryan hated the confines of the small yard of the daycare home where he played after school, and the complete regimentation of our days.

He and I had been happy companions, and now we missed each other. He cried more. So did I. His teacher told us that he talked of Hawaii constantly, and drew pictures of himself and his father boogie boarding in the waves or collecting shells with Cadence.

My life in Hawaii and before had been rich and rewarding, but not in a monetary sense. I had plenty of time to read, study Scripture, garden, and cook. I was the seventies' Earth Mother, baking my own bread, making my own yogurt, sprouting my own sprouts, taking dance classes, and volunteering at the base hospital. I had plans to return to school at some point, but was fascinated by my children, in love with them, really, marveling how like and unlike they were to one another, Jack and me, or our extended family. There was infinite joy in giving them the things in life I'd wanted as a child: a safe and stable home, lots of my time, and the resources to pursue things that interested them, a house full of friends. There had been abundant time too, for Jack and me to talk, listen to music, and discuss world events.

I had let Jack talk me into our buying a house, even though it would mean my going to work. I often deferred to his judgment because he was so often right. It seemed logical and reasonable on the surface: as Jack's rank in the Marines increased, taxes took a larger and larger portion of our income. Both children would be in elementary school. Even though I still hadn't finished a college degree, I had all that medical volunteer experience.

Surely, I could get a job that would help cover the mortgage. I think I made a subconscious and irrational connection to Duane's pushing my mother out of the house those many years ago in Texas, but found no way to articulate that feeling.

I uneasily joined the ranks of the double shift wage earner and homemaker. As Jack's career became increasingly demanding, it was my work to manage the running of the household, from paying the bills, to meal preparation, to managing our children's health and education, everything but the maintenance of the car.

None of these jobs did I hate, in fact, I was far more efficient and capable than he was to manage, enjoy, and even take pride in them. He was never demanding that our home be spotless or that meals appear on any kind of schedule. He took care of his own uniforms and routinely did his own and sometimes the family laundry.

Other than that, I was on my own. In many ways I needed to be, for his work often required that he be away from home: sometimes overnight, sometimes for a week or a month at a time; less often it would require that he be gone for months or be ready to leave us at a moment's notice. Running the household corporation was do-able; running it and holding a job outside my home was another matter. It seemed a cruel shock.

Our family had one car. We'd get up at 05:45AM every day, put the kids, still in their pajamas and slippers, into the car to drop Dad off at the base and come home to hustle our lunches together and ourselves out the door.

I had taken the first job I could land. I became an optician for a group of ophthalmologists in the beach area. It took my whole paycheck to cover our house payment. I walked into the pharmaceutical smell of that office each weekday morning at eight, every female member of the support staff wearing the 'color of the day' with our white lab pants and shoes.

Monday was pink, Tuesday was green, Wednesday was blue, and Thursday was yellow. On Friday, we could wear any of those colors we wanted. Break times and lunch hours were strictly observed; medical chart formats were to be clear and neat. The military had nothing on this place. There was no time to read, to think, to notice the changing of the sky. This was the world of work.

The woman who managed the office had been a single mother for years, a paragon of efficiency and toughness. I liked and admired her very much and felt embarrassed and foolish complaining about my loss of self-determination, the loss of time for myself, and the loss of my funny little boy at home.

I hated my new house every day as I walked out, simply because I had to walk away from it and not return until almost dark. There would be no real garden, no gathering place for the laughing children I had so enjoyed surrounding myself with. It was taking everything I had to own something I had little time to enjoy or even care for.

We made time for church, for outings with the children, making sure they got plenty of daddy-time. We took them to softball league, Girl Scouts, Indian Guides.

There was time for sex, but not for romance, the life of the mind, the theatre, or the concert hall. But it seemed that no one was really suffering but a five-year-old and me, misfits in the stream of career building and economic upward mobility.

"The first time I saw you, I said to myself, 'God, I hope she's not married,'" the man told me that spring. Mark was thin, with sharp features, a mustache, and sad black eyes: a gypsy. The third in a string of optical technicians I'd worked with at the practice, he'd been married for six years, divorced for three, had a son the same age as Bryan.

I had no reason to be attracted to him except for the luxurious notion that he appreciated me, seemed to love my company, and thought me attractive when I so seriously doubted that myself. The chemistry between us, however, stunned me, and sickened me. I thought it would pass, but it didn't. He was a reason to look forward to work. I thought he listened to me when I believed Jack did not. He played the lonely and needy to my listening nurturer. Some physical attraction was there, but far less than the need for attention. I tried to diffuse the feelings by writing a short story about a woman in my predicament, but I was too close to the fire for creativity.

One day, we managed a lunch hour at the same time and took sandwiches to a park near the office where, sitting on a hill pulling up handfuls fragrant grass, I confessed my conflicted feelings for him. How could I be in love with both him, and my husband? I'd never had a twinge of interest in another person ever before in my marriage. He had before. It ruined his first and only marriage, but the romance didn't last. He knew the dangers, but said he had 'special feelings' for me. Without so much the touch of a hand, we left the park and returned to work.

Come to your senses, come to your senses, I'd say in the few moments I had alone with myself, driving to pick up the children or after dropping them off before work. *You're sick. Any man who's unfaithful to his wife would be unfaithful to the next woman. Get over this!*

By the necessity of the workday, I spent more time with Mark those days, however, than I did with my husband. It was he who listened to my analysis of the news, laughed at my jokes, and complimented me on the way I took care of our elderly patients.

A little brush of his fingers on my hair, or a hand on my shoulder, and I'd contemplate what might come next. I could confide in no one except in oblique ways. A woman at my church had just confessed a painful affair. Her friends rallied around her as we helped her talk through her anguish and fears. I lived through her story vicariously, picturing myself in the forbidden excitement of the fateful tryst, the dissolution of my marriage, and seeing the eyes of my hurt and confused children. It seemed as unendurable as my misplaced longing for the kind, lonely man I worked with.

In many ways, Mark was more honorable than I was. I kept saying that we could maintain a heightened friendship, share something between friendship and love, a kind of platonic romance, but I was unbelievably naive about sexuality.

He knew better and wanted a commitment or nothing at all. In spite of my early encounters with my stepfather, I had no real sexual experience before my marriage to Jack, nothing with which to gauge another man's passion. It was incredibly wrong of me to suggest that we continue such a friendship.

I knew I could not betray the man who was the father of my children, who had held me through the healing of the horrified memories of my childhood, had been my best friend, and I loved limitlessly. If I could do that, then I too, could be unfaithful to the next partner. It went against everything I believed.

Many times, I had prayed for wisdom to pull myself together from my perplexing duplicity of heart. The sense that I was nailing the Christ to the cross afresh by entertaining a violation of the promises I had consciously made to Him and my husband insisted itself into my awareness. Passages of scripture I'd studied all my life confronted me with astounding clarity: 'Anyone, then, who knows the good he ought to do and does it not, sins.' Joseph's words to Potiphar's wife kept coming back to me:

'How then could I do such a wicked thing and sin against God?'

Mark and I met alone only once again, and I know it hurt him for me to make the date and then flee in the first moments when we met. I thought about Joseph with Potiphar's wife, I should run and leave my cloak behind, though I was more like Potiphar's wife than the noble Joseph.

I felt cruel and faithless, in fact, I was both. Human. Fallible. Like my own father. The realization burst in upon me, and I thought I could smell my own blood rushing in my head. Of course, my father could still love me and be unfaithful to my mother. Didn't I love my own children? Hadn't he wavered on this same brink?

I did run. If I really loved a person, then I wouldn't put him through a fruitless affair because I knew I'd never end my marriage. If I loved my children enough, then I wouldn't put my need to feel beautiful and desirable ahead of their security. That would be something other than love; it would be giving in to impulses and passions for their own sakes, as interesting and inviting as they may have been at the time.

I begged Mark's forgiveness and hurried home to my house, my son and daughter, my husband. In one week, I found a new job with two ophthalmic surgeons and quit my job at the beach. I was sure that everyone at my office knew why. Half of me wanted Jack to know, the other half could scarcely bear it. He, in fact, had suspected something wrong, but misjudged the man. He thought someone at church was attracted to me.

I didn't hear the body drop to the pavement, but I heard the sound of brakes and the voices of the passersby. Before the first person was in the door to call 911, we were on the phone. The four-doctor ophthalmology practice had their offices in a part of the city known for elderly pedestrians, elderly drivers, many of them needing eye doctors and not knowing it.

I was waiting for Jack to take me to lunch, waiting for Mark to return from his break so that I could go. Mark and Jack had never met; I'd hoped they never would. When I finally made it from the lab to the office door, I saw the two men, the one I'd been tempted to sleep with and the one I slept with every night, in the street kneeling over the form of man with a shock of gray hair. They were moving quickly, talking to one another through what might have been a choreographed act. Sue, the receptionist, was trying to calm Mrs. Friedman, our patient who'd sent the old man to the ground.

"It's going to be all right, sweetie," Sue quietly crooned to the trembling woman, rubbing those diamond-encrusted hands, mottled with age, and knobbed with arthritis.

"I just never saw him. He came from thin air," she cried.

"Let's get you into the office and settled, dear. Jim will pull your car over so the ambulance can get through."

Warmth and brightness startled me as I stepped out of the antiseptic coolness of the office. Everything looked clean. There was no blood; the man appeared motionless, as Jack and Mark worked to revive him.

"She never hit him," a witness said. "Must have scared the old guy to death. Looks like he had 'the big one.'"

Mark's salt and pepper hair glistened in the sun, as he bent over the man. I could see Jack's hands on the man's chest, his wedding ring catching the light. The man's glasses lay in the street, and I went over to pick them up. Fixing glasses. That was my job. Neither Mark nor Jack noticed me, as I inspected the lenses, scratched beyond repair, the frame twisted and broken.

Come on, come on. Let that guy live, I breathed. Two good people were at work on him. One I'd chosen to say good-bye to, one I vowed again to hold onto for the rest of his life, but right then, I just wanted to see the old man move again.

For a moment, I imagined the man's funeral, that we'd all be there, somehow responsible for the moment of his death. I moved closer to see if I knew him, but could only see his shabby, worn clothing. I could hear the paramedics' siren from a few blocks away.

The sound created a panic inside me, and I feared suddenly not only for the man lying in the street, but for my own life, the perilous twists and turns of it. I moved into the shade and turned away from the trio, folding my arms against the side of a car to brace my forehead.

How close I'd come to ruining the life I'd promised myself as a child. None of it would have been fair; all of us would have been hurt. Where does madness like that come from? Jack and I may not have been communicating, but our marriage, our whole family was too precious to mar with infidelity. Mark knew that now, understood it, and quickly made his peace with it.

"He's coming around!" I heard a voice say. A cluster of bystanders hid the scene from me, but the paramedics' vehicle moved in and the siren went blessedly silent.

"Out of the way, please," they ordered, maneuvering their equipment to aid the victim. "Anybody know what happened here?"

I heard my husband's command voice.

"Man's had a heart-attack here, apparently. This fine fellow and I have gotten him back to consciousness, but he's going to need a lot more than we've given him."

I saw the old man then, pale and ghastly, but he was not one of our patients or one of the gentlemen of the neighborhood I often greeted on my lunch-time walks. "Thank you, God. Thank you," I said out loud, but when I did the words caught in my throat. I tried to get a breath, and realized that a cache of tears was about to spill.

"Kay? Honey!"

Jack had suddenly picked me out of the crowd and called to me. His uniform was damp with perspiration, the knees stained from the asphalt. I put my hand up to acknowledge him, as the paramedics were still trying to ask him questions. I sat down on the bench by the jasmine to pull myself together. That jasmine. All those coffee break talks with Mark had been accompanied by that scent of jasmine, in the park, here at the office. But when I smell jasmine today, its fragrance speaks grace to me, a reminder of quite literally coming to my senses. Waves of relief, nausea, fear moved in succession. I put my head between the knees of my white pants. My smock was pink, so it must have been a Monday or Friday. More deep breaths.

"I'm OK. I'm OK," I said, talking out loud to myself again.

"Of course you're OK." A voice and a light hand on my head made me look up.

"Hi, Mark."

"We've got police and paramedics everywhere here. Let's get out of the way."

He was smiling an enigmatic smile at me, as if he were an insider on a great practical joke.

"The guy's going to be OK too," he said.

"Where's Jack?"

"Over there. Said to me, 'Say, mind seeing if my wife's OK over there? The one in the pink smock,' in that official voice of his."

"Dear God."

"Come on. They're almost through with him, and I'll be next."

I pulled in the tears once more, pushing the hair out of my eyes as we walked to where the police were questioning Jack. How many times in the last month had I corked that ocean?

"The right place at the right time, huh?" he asked.

"Two pretty great guys, if you ask me."

"Never thought I'd get to meet your husband that way. Actually, I haven't met him yet. Seems like a hell of a good guy."

"Told you."

"Yeah, I know."

He squeezed my elbow. Somewhere, there was a headache descending.

Part of me never wanted Jack to know I'd been tempted to be unfaithful, another part wanted only to warn him, but not anger or hurt him. He'd have a right to be angry, but I had to make him hear me about the important things. There I was, just like the criminal wanting to be caught, but knowing there'd be hell to pay. There ought to be a better way to make him pay attention. Being a stoic had its downside; if only I could learn to complain effectively, to learn to argue an opinion on my own behalf, not only on behalf of others.

They were bringing Mrs. Friedman outside now, identifying her Lincoln. Sue had calmed her down, and she was returning to her sprightly self. I could almost picture her telling the story at the country club the next day.

"Oh, that poor, poor man. I do hope he'll completely recover."

"They're taking good care of him now, ma'am," an officer said to her.

Order was beginning to reign again on Fanuel Street. The paramedics' van sped away with its precarious patient, and the police were ready to question Mark, looking thinner and taller than ever, as Jack stepped up to him.

"Jack Harkins," he said, firmly taking Mark's bony hand into his own meaty palm. I loved my husband's hands.

"Mark. Good to work with you."

"Oh. This is my wife, Kay. I'm Kay's husband," he reiterated.

"I thought you might be," Mark smiled.

Near that time, I volunteered to go on a weekend camp out with Cadence's new Girl Scout troop. We needed to get away to the mountains, to do girl adventure things together again. After a day of badge earning and an evening of singing, we washed off the sticky sweetness of the s'mores and got ready to turn in. I went to Cadence's tent to say goodnight. She was fully engaged in riotous laughter with her friends, their faces illuminated by flashlight. As she stepped outside for a hug, I held her tightly, breathing in the favorite smell of wood smoke in her hair. Tears came from nowhere.

"What's the matter, Mom?" she asked, looking up surprised at me.

"Oh, I've just missed all this, being with my girl in the fresh air."

"Night, night, Mom," she smiled, giving me an extra squeeze and returning to the giggling warmth of her tent. I stood outside and watched its glow for a moment.

"She's safe," I thought to myself. "We've kept her safe so far from things that hurt us most in our past. God help her for the hurts we can't prevent."

I returned to the little hammock outside my own tent. It was cold, but I climbed into it for a while, letting the net hold me suspended between the damp mossy smell of the earth and the canopy of spring branches above, hanging between doubt and conviction.

How much are we like our parents or their parents before us? Someday, we may find out that our genetic makeup is all we are. Scientists may have already discovered a gene that makes some of us optimistic people no matter what. Just as technology and human insight may be able to engineer away debilitating diseases, we may be able to alter people who may have the weakness of believing in a sovereign God. The world of John Lennon's

'Imagine' could come to pass. On the other hand, if I'd inherited my mother's passive martyrdom and my father's bent toward infidelity, couldn't I engineer my own life away from their costly mistakes? Surely, I was more than just the sum or their parts. Did I believe that free will was a curse, a myth, or a gift from God?

I made a plan to change our lives. I would get out of the medical business and find another home near a college, where I could have a job close to home and more near the cultural and intellectual life I'd always loved, where I could finally, albeit slowly, resume my education. I would make my husband understand that I loved him, but that financial goals couldn't drive our existence. I prayed that I could restore his trust in me.

"Let the bed hold you up," my grandmother used to say when I was fretful and couldn't sleep. As I rested there hearing the sounds of the campsite beginning to die down, I wondered again about my father, about where he'd gone when he'd gone too far.

Are you out there, Daddy? Do you ever wonder what happened to your little girls? I decided to call my sisters the next day to see if they wanted to try to find him.

Chapter Nine

Father Regained

I once asked my grandfather if I could pretend he was my dad for a school event. He turned up his face in laughter, his full head of hair luxuriantly white in the sun.

"That would make me look like quite a sport!" he said.

He was forty the year my mother was born, so I'm sure he pictured the raised eyebrows as a nine-year-old introduced him as her father.

I had gathered for myself quite a collection of father figures by my mid-forties to help make up for missing my own. I had seen my father for the last time when I was nine, before our adoption by my stepfather.

For years after, I studied men twenty years or so older than myself: my friends' fathers, men at church, teachers, or colleagues from work. If they seemed like faithful men, who would never strike a child in anger or cold blood, and made me feel as if I had a brain, I'd befriend them, ask them for advice, and envision what it would be like to introduce them to a room full of people.

In my fiction, he would be on hand for all my important occasions, I'd be on his arm, lightly moving my fingers over the woolly tweed of his jacket in the nervously affectionate way a daughter might.

"Hi. Have you met my Dad yet?"

Although I'd found some admirable substitute fathering when I needed it most, and comforted myself with my faith in God, the Father, there remained a longing each Father's Day, to reconnect with my birth father.

I kept putting off starting a search with a private investigator. My sisters were never too enthusiastic about sharing this quest with me; they had their own families now that stretched their incomes, filled their days, and consumed their love and energies. I once asked my mother what she thought of my trying to find him. From her perpetual cloud of protective cigarette smoke, she gave me one of her standard aphorisms:

"Don't go borrowing trouble. It will probably cost you a fortune. If you ever find him, he'll probably be a bum in the gutter and a drain on your pocketbook for the rest of your life. Go ahead if you want, but I doubt that he's even still alive."

The money again. Why was it always the money?

On the deepest level, I wanted to believe that he had loved me even though he'd perhaps not loved me enough to prevail against the temptations and the circumstances that led him to relinquish me to another father and vanish from my life as he'd been told to.

I needed to establish whether he was alive somewhere, still hoping that one of his three daughters would break through to him from the past. I'd always wondered if he might have tried to force his way through the bureaucracy to find the women whose names had been legally changed at adoption and probably at marriage. I'd toyed for years with hiring a private detective to look for him, but found it expensive and risky. What if he were dead? No father, no possibility of reclamation.

I was nearly forty-five, when I discovered an article in one of those grocery store check-out lane magazines, the kind that usually have a dichotomy of 'Sure-fire weight loss tips!' and killer chocolate cake on the covers.

Perhaps there'd been an attractive table setting, or time management teaser there to make me want to put it in my basket; I can't remember actually purchasing it. But in that issue, I discovered that the Social Security Administration will forward a letter to a missing person: someone who's owed some money, or needs to be contacted for a medical or financial reason, or someone being sought for some other humanitarian reason. They won't tell you where the person is, or even if the person ever receives your letter, that's confidential. But if you send as much information as you can, they'll track the person through their system and deliver your message to them. I clipped the small column and put it in my planner book where it stayed for months.

On the afternoon of Father's Day, 1991, I sat in the basement of a friend's home I was sharing while completing my Master's degree near Washington, DC. My husband had already gone ahead to Florida on his assignment for the post-Gulf War period. My daughter and son were back in San Diego, preparing to complete their respective senior years of college and high school, where I would return in August to teach writing full-time while they finished school.

As I sat with my computer screen against the newly painted walls of my friend's basement guest quarters, a summer downpour sent noisy waterfalls over the eaves into the flowerbeds framed in the windows above me that I often opened ever so slightly to let in the aromatherapy of wet soil and greenery.

If you think you're a writer, I said to myself out loud, and you're going to tell people that writing can make a difference, then try it on your own seeming impossibilities.

In what a friend would later call the most selfish act of my life, I composed the following letter, being careful to include details that would let him know it could only come from me:

June 14, 1991.

To Mr. Paul Hubert Leighty,

For many years, I have thought about how to contact you. I recently read that the Social Security Administration would forward letters to people. I have so little information about you; I hope that this letter will find its way to you.

Dear Daddy,

This letter is not meant to intrude upon your life or ask anything of you, but for many years, I have wanted to tell you that I am out here and well and that I think of you often, although it has been over thirty years since I have seen you. I have never stopped loving you, and have believed that you always have loved me, no matter what anyone told me. The memories I have of you are of happy and sad times. But I always remember how you could make us laugh and believe that everything would be all right. I remember being a very small girl with pajama feet that were too large for me, so you used to call me "wabbit foot." Somehow, precious memories like these have been a comfort to me in lonely and confusing times.

I am now almost forty-five years old. I have a wonderful husband and two children who are almost grown. I will have been married for twenty-two years on the 4th of July. After raising my kids, I'm now finishing my master's degree in English and will be a college professor in the fall.

My sisters, Janis and Susan, are both well and happily married also, each with two children and fine husbands. The years between the time you last saw us and the time we married and started our own lives were difficult and sometimes heartbreaking. God was very faithful to us all and saw us through troubles and dangers. For my own part, I know that the love and faith I was taught to have from my mother's parents and your parents, especially your dear mother, Helen, sustained me through many dark hours. While I am no longer a Catholic, I cherish my early learning and upbringing in that church and believe that it adds a great deal to my present spiritual life.

I have always prayed that you have found a happy life and family and that you are loved by those near you. It would bring me great joy to hear from you. But again, not for one moment would I wish to disrupt or make uncomfortable the life and family you may have now after all these years. If you choose not to respond to this letter, I will understand completely. Just know that I do think of you with love and pray for you. If you would like to write to me, I will be at the above address until August 1st. After that time, you may write me at the following address in California...

Again, I would love to hear from you. God bless you and keep you.

I didn't have very much information to send to the SSA, just my father's full name, the full names of his parents and that he'd served in the Army in World War II. My mother couldn't remember his birthday, and certainly not his Social Security number. I proved to myself that writing could be cathartic but not necessarily therapeutic.

As I probed my memories to include those small details that would let this man know that the letter could only have come from his oldest daughter, I pushed the tears away and typed with wet fingers. Proofing the letter a few times during the rest of the day, I tried to decide whether or not to send it.

Perhaps it was just a good device to evoke some characters for the short story I was trying to write, a little exercise on the way to something else. I wrote a cover letter to the SSA, explaining my purpose and thanking them for whatever efforts they could produce on my behalf. The next morning, without allowing myself much time to reconsider, I mailed the letters and spent the day reading a hundred pages of a linguistics journal in the damp coolness of my downstairs hermitage.

The summer term ended, I got my degree, and Jack took me to Maine for a week as a celebration, before we began another eight months of professional separation. He liked to say that we had a 'bi-coastal marriage,' laughing that this phrase romanticized our pragmatic decision to live apart for a year.

I preferred to say that we were 'professionally separated,' suspecting that my feminist friends would smile on such a term, although he objected that it sounded as if a doctor had recommended that we put a distance between us.

On a rainy summer morning, we lay in the room of our bed and breakfast, the window open, and a piney breeze lightly misting our sheets. His usually prickly-short Marine Corps haircut was growing out to the vacation length I preferred, so I rubbed my hands on his head.

"This is a close as I'll ever get to running my fingers through your hair, isn't it?"

"You never know. I could move up here someday and become a hairy mountain man."

"Why can't I quite picture that?" I smiled a cheesy smile.

A stronger insistence of breeze pushed more mist into our lazy conversation and a scent of soil, rain, and greenery took me back for an instant to my summer basement home. I suddenly couldn't remember telling Jack about my inquiry. How could I forget?

"Did I ever tell you that I sent a letter through the Social Security Administration to look for my father?"

"Yes, of course you did. While you were at back in Fairfax. All those books have made you senile. What ever became of that?"

"Nothing. Not a word. My mom is probably right that he's dead."

"Don't think that yet. You're dealing with a government bureaucracy, here. They probably haven't even opened the envelope. That letter is still in a big bag somewhere."

Now he was rubbing my head, pushing the hair out of my face, pulling me back into the contentment of the moment.

"Hmm," I said, as I drifted back to sleep. It was always like that: fears comforted, almost dismissed. He'd hold me when I would let one piece or another of abuse or loss out into the light. Just as I never pressed him for revelations about Vietnam, he'd never question me for more details than I would spill at one time. He'd never tell me to stop crying, but let me pound or scream out the grief and anger until I could again hold it at bay or it was diffused by the exposure. He had found a faithful wife, and I had found a patient lover.

We learned we could go on with the lives we purposed, keeping the horrors of war and my demented stepfather in their proper places in the past, by working through the memories as they came up and savoring the peace and happiness of the present. The venture with the letter left my head again for months as I prepared for my first college teaching assignment.

The sunrays bounced off the ocean and filled my little apartment on the campus one October afternoon, as I sat writing comments on a batch of freshman composition essays. I'd received a letter from the Social Security Administration three days before that began, "Thank you for your inquiry. We are forwarding your letter to the person you have requested. Please remember that we cannot notify you of this person's whereabouts or confirm the receipt of your document." My husband had been right again. What a backlog.

When the phone rang, I was sure it was my son's girlfriend wondering why he wasn't home from school yet, but I answered it on the second ring. The department secretary's strained voice was on the line.

"Kay? Are you sitting down, honey?" She paused and swallowed in her characteristic and dramatic way. "I just had a man on the phone who said he is your father and he hasn't seen you for thirty-six years. He started to cry and asked me if I would call and ask if it was OK for him to call you at your apartment. He's waiting for me to call him back."

"Oh, please just give me his number, Sharon. I'll call him myself right now. After all these months. No, all these years. Dear God."

"Are you OK with this? Do you want me to come down?"

"No. No, I'm fine. Thanks for being his go-between. I'll call you and tell you what happens. Please, just let me have the number he gave you."

Through sighs and sniffles, the self-appointed mother figure of the lit department gave me a phone number in New Orleans. How had he gotten there from Des Moines?

"Oh, sweetie, he was just crying and crying when I told him you worked here in our department. He almost seems afraid to talk to you."

"It's OK, Sharon. I know I'll cry, and I'm almost afraid to talk to him too, but let me call him now. I promise to tell you what happens."

Part of me wanted to call Jack first, but I couldn't be sure I would reach him on the East Coast. This man, who said he was my father, who I was certain was my father, was sitting by a silent telephone, waiting for pieces of a puzzle to be snapped into place. I pressed the numbers carefully.

"Hello, Dad. It's Mary Kay."

"Oh… Oh." Silence.

"It's me, Daddy. Are you all right?"

I listened, as he struggled with his breath through the sound of his tears, but he soon regained his composure. "Yes, yes, I'm OK now. I can't tell you how much it means to have gotten this letter."

In the half-hour that ensued, I tried to construct the father who had remained a mystery to me. His deep voice sounded young, but nothing as I had imagined. Of all the sounds and images I'd stored away, I had no memory of that voice; I could not picture him as he must have been at that moment.

He asked me about my mother and my sisters, about my children and my husband, about my sisters' children and husbands. Then, as we began to talk about one another, layers of time melted away, perhaps because I had willed it, perhaps because he did.

"And, you know, I've become a writer in my old age," he told me.

"A writer? How long have you been a writer?"

"Oh, about the last five or six years."

"Me too, Dad, me too."

We laughed at the ironies. He related a little story or two about my childhood.

"You were always the smartest little girl. Everybody said you were smart, not just your Dad."

Smart. Of all the descriptors of me, smart had rarely been one of them. In the positive sense, I'd been called

154

capable, helpful, organized, and even knowledgeable. According to the old tapes in my head, I was still sloppy, dull, fat, lazy, and selfish. But now, my own father was telling me again that I had been smart all along.

"My precious baby girl, you were smart enough to find me," he kept saying over and over. "I started to try to find you so many times. Mary, my wife now, has been trying to get me to put this to rest for years. I've prayed for you three girls every day of my life."

My astonishment came in waves. I already had a full garden in my heart with our family, our friends, my work, those other father figures I'd found for myself, but my selfishness had prevailed. The one withered, un-watered corner of my heart soaked in his words and rose into bloom. After all I'd lost and gained, now I was being given more. I was, in fact, smart enough to find my father for the price of a postage stamp.

I agreed to call my sisters and give them his number should they choose to call him as well. Janis, four years younger than I, had always been his favorite, which was fine with me. It was she who had suffered the worst abuse by our stepfather after I left for college, and she who would need her own dad the most. His restoration to her was life-giving. Susan, who'd been six weeks old the day of my parents' divorce, was only four the year we were adopted. She had no recollection of him. Janis called him that day; Susan chose to write to him later.

I got Jack on the phone right after I told my father that I would call him back soon, in the next day or so, after he'd perhaps had a chance to speak with Janis or Susan.

"After all this time, honey, you have your own father back. I'm so proud of you," he'd said.

I kept pressing my fingers to my face as we talked. They were cold, but my face was burning hot. It must have been scarlet, it felt scarlet. Did I feel embarrassed, guilty? I suddenly sensed that it was because finding my father seemed much less momentous to me than it had to my father. I was the safe one for so long, he the one still in torment. Now, I had something I'd wanted all along. I'd been right, right. He'd rued the day he let my stepfather adopt us, he'd never stopped loving us or hoping to find us again one day. I could almost let him go again.

"I told him how wonderful you are, Jack. I told him how incredible your family has been to me. They were family enough, and now this. How will we make room for him?" I asked.

He laughed. "How does anyone make room for a new baby or a new brother-in-law? You love them and let them grow on you."

I'm sure that's what his family had done with me.

My children were happy for me, delighted too, it seemed, with their mother's ingenuity, but my son denied any curiosity in meeting his new grandfather.

"I only need one grandfather," he declared, "and I've already got the best one." His resolution startled me at first, until I recalled myself making similar statements about my father-in-law. "Jack Harkins, Senior. Who needs another father with a guy like that?" I'd often bragged. My husband's parents had taken me in and loved me as they would their own child.

I tried to share the news of my reclaimed father with at least some level of reserve. It seemed melodramatic, absurd, and unbelievable; the stuff of Unsolved Mysteries or This is Your Life, although I did have the urge to hang a big, yellow banner over my apartment balcony that read, 'It's a daddy!'

Students in my classes burst into tears when I told the story the next day. In fact, almost everyone was moved to weeping as Sharon had been, and it surprised me every time. I did not cry until three months later, when I, at last, saw my father face to face. In the days following our first phone conversation, I simply felt a puzzling and frightening new strength, a dense calm. I'd done without him for so long, it was suddenly difficult but beautiful to imagine how I could fit this new man into my already full life.

My reunion with him came in January. Friends asked us if we planned to call in the media, but the thought repulsed me. I had a professional conference already scheduled in Tampa and had planned to spend time with Jack on the same trip. I asked my father to fly from New Orleans and meet us, because I needed Jack to be there with me when I saw him again. Unfoundedly, I feared being alone with my own father.

There were no crowds in the terminal that afternoon, the floors polished, and the piped-in music nondescript. My father by then had sent a photograph of himself, tall, with a tidy salt-and-pepper beard (a writer's beard, he'd called it) and not enough hair for the crew cut of my childhood memories. Jack saw him first.

"There he is, honey. I think that's him." He took me by the arm, the same way he would always do when escorting me at any military occasion.

"I see him, I see him."

My dad had chosen a sweater and a tweed coat for the trip. I wore a white cotton sweater and red skirt. Jack released my arm as my father recognized me and I ran to him. People stopped and stared as I held his hands and then his face, as tears finally poured down my own.

"My little girl, my little girl!" he kept repeating as we embraced.

Jack had taken his carry-on bag and stood protectively as the embarking passengers too, had eyes filled with emotion.

I suddenly realized that my father was trembling uncontrollably and Jack caught him by the arm as he'd held me before.

"Let's duck over here for a drink, Paul. I'm Jack. So great to see you at last. It'll be a while before the baggage is out anyway."

As a threesome, with my dad in the middle, we found the nearest terminal restaurant and slid into a circular upholstered booth. The next three days, between the sessions of my conference and over breakfasts and dinners, we pieced together our paths over the intervening years.

How he'd gone to New Mexico with the woman he'd had the affair with and it had fallen apart in months, his return to Des Moines and problems finding a job and his failure to reconcile with my mother in spite of my grandfather's encouragement.

"I don't blame her for being so damned mad. I was a young fool then. As a matter of a fact, I was a damned fool for a long time," he told me.

There were his other marriages, one to an alcoholic, and another to a woman with bi-polar illness. I had a half-sister who lived in Norfolk, Virginia, the daughter of the alcoholic who committed suicide. He'd found his Mary just six years before, and his life had made a significant shift. He was writing mystery books now, playing golf, but still selling resort real estate. Mary had been trying to get him to find us.

We asked one another question after question; he regaled Jack with stories from the war. He'd been on Iwo Jima with his army unit, the same time as the Marines.

"You girls found yourselves some fine husbands," he would say. "Your mom sure did a fine job of raising you."

"God looked out for them, Paul," Jack replied. "And Jerry, Kurt, and me too!"

Jack and I would trade a little head shaking look and a wry smile that said, "If he only knew."

It only took a short time after I found him, before the ripples of my recovered father began to make their changes, some of them painful, some of them joyful, some of them perplexing. There was the problem of my mother who had been living with Janis in Maryland for over a year. My sister recounted the hour after I had called mother to tell her that I had reconnected with my father.

"You should have seen her, Mary Kay. She howled and cried and beat her fists against her knees. 'He's married. Married! I never stopped loving him, now I'll never have him,' she kept saying. My God, she hasn't had a good word for him for thirty-six years, and now she thinks he'd come back and sweep her off her feet? I wanted to slap her out of it, but I know it was a shock."

I was stunned, flabbergasted. This was the woman whose anger burned so hot that she had my father arrested for kidnapping when he picked me up from school on my seventh birthday. The woman who had refused my grandfather's repeated pleas for reconciliation when my father came to him sorrowful for his immature infidelity. The woman who swore her best friends to secrecy about our address when she remarried and we moved to Texas. The woman who was somehow paralyzed for more than a decade against taking any action against the monstrous behavior on the part of her second husband.

She, who wouldn't subject her daughters to the immorality of our own father's unfaithfulness, but practically lived in bigamy until my poor sister tried to commit suicide. Now she raged like the widow at a murder, unable to take any joy in her daughters' newfound doting father. What had I done?

Within months, as my middle sister blossomed in the sunshine of my father's love, my mother could not bear to stay in Janis' home and moved to North Carolina to be near Susan, who, because she had almost no memory of him, kept our father at a polite distance.

In those October days of re-connection, our father turned out to be magnanimous and charming about my mother, effusive in his praise of what he had taken to be the courageous and loving upbringing of their daughters in spite of his errant ways.

In a phone call he made to her in the days after our own phone reunion, he disarmed our mother totally, left her with nothing to rage about and much to ponder. While he made it clear that he was finally, happily, and firmly married to his fourth wife, he took responsibility for his wrongdoing; he apologized for giving up and allowing the lawyers to talk him into our adoptions.

The war had robbed him of his adolescence and he had behaved as one for many years after his betrayal of her; he was ashamed of his cowardice and his abandonment of her and his daughters. He thanked her for her loving care of us, the wonderful daughters, wives, and mothers, she had so clearly helped us to become. What could she say?

He soothed her romantic heart, declaring that she had been his first love and he could never forget that. He named the songs that had been 'their songs' and told her that whenever he heard them, he remembered her with fondness and without rancor. I believe those words started her down the slow, painful, but sure path of healing.

She had no choice now but to admit to herself the cost of her anger and the depth of her deception. Telling herself the truth began finally, ironically, to ease her self-loathing and send her toward grace. Who knows if my father's declarations were to let him off the hook with honesty or because he genuinely felt these things for her?

It was many months before I was able speak to him in careful, small increments about the kinds of evil her husband worked on us. It was only when I was able to share a working manuscript of the book I was writing about my childhood that he would come to know the full effect of one disastrous marriage after another. I thought he might be distraught, but he remained philosophical: nothing could be changed now, and my sisters and I would not have the loving husbands and families we now had.

He would not have his loving wife, Mary, or his other daughter, Terry. He had to turn away from the past, repent of his sins, and go on in love. He found himself able to absolve my mother from her complicity in our abuse. He seemed to understand what she had confessed to us when she finally woke up and divorced Duane. She had not been able bear the shame of another failure in marriage, could not return herself and her daughters to the poverty she had perceived when she fended for us on her own.

Most of the time, I can subscribe to his philosophy. Even as I child, I had pondered that if one second of history were altered, everything would be different. It's always a gamble to wonder what other outcomes there could have been. Perhaps, we'd have become spoiled, ungrateful, rebellious daughters, but maybe we'd have become concert pianists, artists, Broadway dancers or nuns.

What if I'd fought against Duane and been sent to the Buckner Children's Home as he had bluffed and had become separated from my mother and sisters? What if I'd just had the guts to have gotten my sisters and me the hell out of there, as many people felt I was too weak and cowardly to do?

Finally, I decided that there was no reason to even consider the 'what if' questions, and not moving ahead in forgiveness would be giving Duane's harmful old power continued life in the present. Everyone must be forgiven, including Duane.

I have to remind myself of that every time the poison of angry remembrance or resentment returns. I do have the right to remember, the right to name the wrongs done to my mother, my sisters, my half-brother, my father, and to me. I have the right to bear witness, but not to judge, if I wish to be judged in love and compassion for my own evils and shortcomings. Not to forgive would be to continue to bring needless suffering into what the love of God might put to rest. Not to forgive is to deny the beauty and safety of the present moment, and the moment of presence when redemption is at hand.

Chapter Ten
What Remains

In his book, Drawing Life: Surviving the Unabomber, artist and scientist, David Gelernter, posits that once some act of evil is perpetrated, a thousand acts of kindness rush in to its wake. Along with our right to name crime, horror, and suffering, we must also bear witness to acts of mercy.

There's a mass shooting; someone, many someones, show themselves to be heroically self-sacrificial. A famine, and the poorest of the poor will offer her last scrap of food to a starving child. Ordinary people risk life and limb to rescue others from the flames of wildfires. In a concentration camp, one prisoner takes the punishment of another. These acts don't justify, don't sanctify, and often don't even assuage the suffering caused by the evil. They are the embodiment, the incarnation, if you will, of the love that permeates the foundation of the still dynamic universe. God, who is love and mercy has created us for love and mercy and gives us the capacity to act from divine energy in the face of evil.

I hope that I will never require being tortured for this belief. But it is the irrefutable fruit of my admittedly limited experience with human suffering. Too many times I have been the recipient of this kind of love from unexpected places and unlikely people, too many times I have been its witness. Of course, you don't get the ticket until you get on the train, but should I be tortured, I vow to cling to this good news, this gospel: God is ever with us, as close as our own breath, most often in inexplicable ways.

I know a woman of Jewish background, who, having been ruthlessly, mercilessly abused by her own mother, recounts a childhood dream, vision, or experience (she still cannot be sure which) of being comforted by The Christ of whom she had barely heard.

My little sister, years after our harrowing life with Duane, related to me the same vision/dream I had myself: being gathered into the lap of Jesus for comfort and consolation. At the time of our suffering, we were unable to speak even to one another of such things, to even admit to one another what we suffered, thinking that we alone were chosen for that particular affliction, that maybe we deserved it, or told that we'd be killed for revealing its source.

How often we, my sisters, my mother, did not recognize the Stockholm syndrome-like power that kept us closed off, blind, wishing, perhaps even thinking that what transpired to us and around us was not even happening. We eventually asked and gave forgiveness to one another; we sometimes found it much harder to forgive ourselves. But angels abounded in one form or another, and we lived to testify.

School had always been a safe haven for me, a place to shine, and junior high was no exception; angels did abound there. Mr. Alton, the science teacher, who let me assist him the lab after school because I rode the last bus that left in the afternoon, like my grandfather, spoke to me as if I had intelligence.

Mr. Davis, the band director, helped me with my music because he knew my parents wouldn't allow lessons. With clearest remembrance, I can return to the moment Mrs. Chambers of 8th grade English, took my hands in hers one afternoon, as I talked to her about my homework assignment.

"Why are these hands shaking, Mary Kay?"

I looked down at her hands, large, soft, and manicured, around mine, never noticing that my own shook until that moment. I tried to memorize that look in her eyes.

"I don't know. I mean, I didn't know. Do they shake all the time?"

"I just notice it sometimes, sweetie. Do you eat breakfast every day?" she asked.

I told her that I did. Eating well was not a problem at our home.

"Is there anything wrong at your house? Is anyone sick or hurt there?" she asked.

I shook my head no. Who could begin to share something so dangerous? As much as I longed to beg for help for my sisters and me, I feared whatever hell might break loose should some 'intruder' again come to our door. It was enough that someone had seen and sought to touch my suffering.

I took note of her manner, her voice. I vowed I would be that way, someday. I would learn to look with those eyes.

Love/God comes to us in beauty, in art, in literature, most of the time quite obliquely, unobtrusively, sometimes hidden or forgotten, until a much later revelation, when a refrain of music or a fragrance will momentarily reverse time, tearing away the present to reveal a face, a locale, or a long forgotten thought or emotion.

Such was an occasion for me on a visit to Scotland, when an odd rending of that curtain would occur for me as I read again, for the sake of scholarship, a passage from Jane Eyre, a novel I had loved during my years as the pliant, complacent stepdaughter.

By the fire in a modest country manor house, I read the words, 'I should have my unblighted self to turn to.'

Wait. I dropped the book as I immediately returned to my fourteen-year-old self, carrying with me for weeks a dog-eared paperback copy of Jane Eyre. I remembered myself copying this phrase into the makeshift diary of the blank pages in the backs of my flute method books, where no parental eyes would think to pry.

I recognized now in the words I was reading a kind of clue, an answer to the questions others had often asked me and I had asked myself about how I had endured, even hidden the pathology of our family. Evidently, I had scrawled the words of the fictional Jane not only into my book, but also into my psyche.

I should still have my unblighted self to turn to: my natural unenslaved feelings with which to communicate in moments of loneliness. There would be recesses in my mind which would be only mine to which he never came; the sentiments growing there fresh and sheltered, which his austerity could never blight, nor his measured warrior-march trample down.

The passage was a completely loose association between my own life in the context of the novel, unmoored to it even, but suddenly I remembered reading those sentences to myself many times when tempted to live out Duane's disparaging expectations of me, just as I might repeat verses of scripture in my head.

I went back to the beginning of the novel and read it yet again, with astonished eyes: I had made role models of Jane and her poor dying friend, Helen Burns. Helen had talked sense to little Jane when she had been infuriated with unjust and harsh treatment. Helen was at peace with her own faults and her advice to Jane not to trust too much in others' opinion made sense to me, as well as to Jane.

My own unblighted self was that kid on that long-ago November bank, known and loved. My teenage self somehow still knew that. The rock of that old revelation of oneness and a place at the table of divine love had somehow kept protecting me. Perhaps, that is why Christ said that the kingdom of heaven belongs to little children. If I could keep remembering who I thought was and to whom I truly belonged to, perhaps I could survive, and if I could to go on to live a life that I would choose for myself.

At the Brian Center in Monroe, North Carolina, nearly every week a church group came to sing the old hymns with the residents of the plain, garden variety nursing home/rehabilitation center. In the minutes before ten o'clock, the slow line of wheelchairs, like a parade of escargot, eased into the large room with the polished floor, the room where the boring food was served every day, where they gathered in to the Bingo games for which my mother was known to be the all-time winner, where now everyone lined up in front of the old upright piano and the battered hymnal was opened to the first tune of the day. For fifteen years after my mother's catastrophic stroke in 2001, I came from California for several days, each year to share in the sameness of her days.

Susan, who visited her nearly every day of the year, bore the years-long responsibility for her care; I came for my few days of celebrity as Ruth's daughter from California. I knew I could not make up for the time I was unable to give my mother throughout the year. Each year as I left, I could barely breathe with the understanding that I may have seen her for the last time.

But my mom was a trooper. Having hidden her high blood pressure for at least six years because she was sure a doctor would try to make her quit smoking, she fell out of her chair one February afternoon while doing the handwork on her granddaughter's wedding dress in a stroke that would leave her paralyzed on the right side of her body, that would rob her of ever creating meaningful speech again in her life.

The blocked pathway of language from the brain to the hand or the tongue would rob us of hearing any more stories of her young life, of her parents or brothers. She could not speak, she could not write, what she meant to say, she could not type. All verbal narrative we could have received from her was severed forever and replaced with only the ability to answer yes or no.

She barely survived the stroke. She could not speak, could not swallow, and was fed through a tube into her stomach for six months. When she rallied, the previously anxious woman emerged cheerfully defiant of death. The constant worrier transformed into 'Happy Ruthie,' the smiling joy bringer of the Brian Center.

"I wouldn't have given a plug nickel for your mamma's life when she come in here," a fellow resident told me one year. "Now you look at her, smiling her way down the hallway every day."

Smiling, indeed, alternately waving a left handed greeting to all with pushing the left wheel of her chair. Neither her doctors nor we knew what gave her the will to revive and live yet another fifteen years with her limited capacities.

In the week following the stroke, we gathered around her bed in the hospital. The doctors encouraged us to get her to sing to try to open up her path to language. With Broca's aphasia, a person cannot generate original speech, but may be able to create any language that may be in the memory in the form of a song or poem.

"Sing to her. Get her to sing with you," was the doctor's order. And so, we sang ballads, old patriotic songs. Visitors in the hallway stopped at our door as her three daughters sang the show tunes she valiantly mouthed along with us to keep her breathing going, to try to help her sing her way back to life.

So the hymn singing was always a highlight of my visits to our mother, joining in her animated renditions of the evergreens from the beat-up Baptist hymnal. Everybody knew what would come at the end. Susan, our mother, and I would sing our trio of 'In the Garden,' Mom's favorite hymn. There was never a dry eye in the crowd, including our own many times.

There's a verse from the Psalms to the effect that God lives in the praise of His people, and the moments when we sang together in the dining hall or on the wide porches of the center formed the heart of our communication, our unity, our oneness in what we had survived.

In our hours on the porch or in my mother's room during my visits, I would ask her yes/no questions about our family history, her history. In spite of her physical and linguistic limitations, she remained extraordinarily alert and aware of everything around her, even as her hearing began to decline.

With Susan, and to a good extent with Janis and me, she was a keen player of that yes/no game of charades. Once on an outing to Wal-Mart, she was able to help us sleuth out that she was looking a pack of playing cards. Imagine us in the center of the huge store asking her the questions it took to narrow down her desired purchase.

Together, we achieved our objective in a little over five minutes. Asking her questions about her childhood in Massachusetts or years our grandfather did floral work in Des Moines was more work. Because she could not tell us what year or in what place something happened, we had to ask our questions quite specifically.

"Was it in 1957 that Grandpa taught that class at the University of Iowa?" or "Uncle Frank was in the Navy in the war, wasn't he?" She was unfailingly patient with us and with herself, but there was much we wanted to know that we were never able to discover. When Janis found a trove of old photographs, there was no way for our mother to tell us or for us to ask the names and relationships of the people in the photos. We tried to make good notes to piece together our family story.

My mother passed away on her own mother's birthday, the summer before she would turn 91. My father had celebrated his 91st birthday that same month. The only 'funeral' she wanted was a family reunion to be planned in the autumn of the year after she died, at the place in the Great Smokey Mountains she loved the most. She had made my sister promise her this on their yearly camping trips before the stroke.

My daughter and I decided that we would make a visit to my father at his home in the green valleys of Tennessee on our way to the memorial reunion in North Carolina.

My father too, had retained a keen mind into his ninth decade, and enjoyed surprisingly good health for his years in the care of his dear Mary.

Cadence was feeling that same pressing need to capture as much of her grandfather's story from him in the few days we had with him, and he was only too glad to oblige her journalist's questions. My dad had the gift of gab, having sold real estate all his life, and possessed a love of storytelling displayed in his quirky murder mysteries. We whiled away the hours of that visit, avoiding the gulf between his politics and ours, with stories of the war, his old friends, and the sad stories of the middle two of his four wives. One of his favorite stories was of me finding him, and the story of his first meeting with Cadence. She is one of few people on earth who can say the first time she saw her grandfather was in Las Vegas where he bought her a martini.

On our drive away from Tennessee and into the mountains, we concluded that my father might well have been one of the most fortunate men we knew, having survived a terrible war, three divorces, and the loss and regaining of more than one fortune. His aging years were spent with a woman he adored and who adored him. He played golf until two weeks before we lost him that same year, before the Christmas holiday.

My parents, my grandparents, my beloved Inez and Jack Senior, and our tormentor, Duane, are all gone from this dimension of life now. Yet they remain with us, just across that thin boundary between life and death, their stories and our stories still part of the fabric of all that has come before and all that is yet to be. My choice is to continue to forgive, to continue to learn the childhood lesson given when heaven and earth merged in a bank of leaves in Iowa. I can always run to silence, run to love, because we live, and move, and have our being in it.

Every once in a while, I'll put on some music and spin myself out again to eternity, out into that curve of time, both like and unlike our own. Suffering and humiliation, guilt and redemption, forgiveness and healing become more than words. They are seen in the briefest but not insignificant moments of reading and understanding, in shaking hands held still, in unbroken promises of fidelity, clean sheets, hot water, a sudden recognizing of my own sin in that of another. In the depth of such prayer, I watch myself there on my knees, then in the room, in the house, the city, the continent, the planet, with all those who have screamed in pain, bled, and died, who have laughed, enfolded a lover, kissed a baby. We are held in the infinite love and grace of the God, seen and unseen, who is always there ahead of us, always immediately with us, when we have the awareness to notice. The picture can only be borne for a few seconds, but it is enough to hold me.